Find the Errors!

PROOFREADING ACTIVITIES

Nancy Lobb

J. WESTON
WALCH
PUBLISHER

Portland, Maine

User's Guide
to
Walch Reproducible Books

As part of our general effort to provide educational materials which are as practical and economical as possible, we have designated this publication a "reproducible book." The designation means that purchase of the book includes purchase of the right to limited reproduction of all pages on which this symbol appears:

Here is the basic Walch policy: We grant to individual purchasers of this book the right to make sufficient copies of reproducible pages for use by all students of a single teacher. This permission is limited to a single teacher, and does not apply to entire schools or school systems, so institutions purchasing the book should pass the permission on to a single teacher. Copying of the book or its parts for resale is prohibited.

Any questions regarding this policy or requests to purchase further reproduction rights should be addressed to:

Permissions Editor
J. Weston Walch, Publisher
321 Valley Street • P. O. Box 658
Portland, Maine 04104-0658

1   2   3   4   5   6   7   8   9   10

ISBN 0-8251-3724-1

Copyright © 1987, 1998
J. Weston Walch, Publisher
P. O. Box 658 • Portland, Maine 04104-0658

Contents

To the Teacher .... *v*

To the Student .... *vii*

Using Your Learning Style for Better Proofreading ...... *viii*

Find the Errors! Pretest 1

1. Let's Be Proper! 6
2. What a Capital Idea! 8
3. Another Capital Idea! 8
4. Capital Letter Practice 12
5. Put an End to That! 14
6. Time for a Break! 16
7. More Break Time! 16
8. What Did He Say? 20
9. Some Troublemakers 22
10. The Versatile Apostrophe 24
11. Punctuation Practice 26
12. Practice Makes Perfect! 26
13. Review Time 26
14. Peaceful Coexistence 31
15. Principal Problems with Principal Parts 34
16. Puzzling Pronouns 36
17. Dangling Modifiers 38
18. Mystifying Modifiers 40
19. Practice Those Principles! 43
20. More Principle Practice 43
21. Proofreading Practice 43
22. The Incomplete Thought 47
23. A Word Traffic Jam 49

24. Proofreading for Sentence Sense 51

25. The Spice of Life 53

26. What's the Correct Time? 55

27. Give It Life! 57

28. Weeding Out Wordiness 60

29. Be Original! 62

30. Practice Your Style 64

31. More Stylish Review 64

32. Perfect Your Style 64

33. Where's the Proof? 64

34. School Daze 70

35. Proofreader's Delight 72

36. Positively Proofread! 72

37. Proofreading Crossword Puzzle 75

Find the Errors! Posttest 77

Proofreading Checklist 81

To the Teacher

How to Use This Book

Find the Errors! is an easy and effective way to help your students improve their writing skills. Students will enjoy reading the humorous anecdotes in each exercise and locating the errors. By the time they have completed all the exercises, knowing what writing errors to avoid has been reinforced over and over. Being able to proofread to eliminate their own errors will improve the students' written work.

Find the Errors! is a reproducible teacher book containing both student sections and teacher material. Reproducible student material includes 37 exercises and both a pretest and posttest on the contents of *Find the Errors!* Reproducible pages are identified by the copyright line with a flame logo at the bottom. They can be copied and distributed to each student. For each reproducible student exercise, a teacher page provides background information on grammar usage for the topic to be presented, an answer key, and additional activities pertaining to the student exercise(s) that follow.

The Reproducible Student Exercises

The proofreading exercises are divided into two areas of writing skills: mechanics and problem-sentence revision. The mechanics section includes units on capitalization and punctuation. The problem-sentence revision section includes units on usage, sentence structure, and style. Each unit contains a number of exercises relating to its particular topic. These are followed by several review exercises that include all topics previously considered.

Each exercise in *Find the Errors!* also contains five spelling errors for students to locate and correct. The purpose of the spelling words is to help students learn to recognize common spelling errors. The words chosen for this purpose are not long, difficult words. Rather, they are simple words with which many students nonetheless have difficulty. Each spelling word falls into one of three categories:

1. Words that are often confused, such as *who's* and *whose*, *choose* and *chose* or *all together* and *altogether*.

2. Words that illustrate basic spelling rules, such as *receive* ("*i* before *e* . . .") or *skies* ("change the *y* to *i* and add *es*").

3. Words taken from various lists of "spelling demons." Examples of these words are *tomorrow*, *eighth*, and *ninth*.

The Pretest and Posttest

A proofreading pretest and posttest have been included in the package for assessment purposes. The pretest may be used to determine specific areas in which students have difficulty. In addition, it may be used in conjunction with the posttest as an evaluation tool.

Each item in both tests exemplifies one or more major writing errors. Each writing error has been correlated in the Answer Key with the exercises in *Find the Errors!* which teach that writing skill.

The Teacher Guide Pages

A teacher guide page precedes every student activity or group of activities in *Find the Errors!* Each teacher guide page contains a detailed explanation of the rules included in that particular writing skill area. For example, in the capitalization unit, all the rules of capitalization are listed and explained in the section called "Background Information." The teacher guide pages also include complete answer keys and suggestions for additional activities. These include activities for enrichment, additional practice, and student writing projects. Multicultural, hands-on, and cooperative learning activities comprise a large segment of these extensions.

Provision for Individual Differences

A section entitled "Using Your Learning Style for Better Proofreading" (p. *viii*) gives students suggested methods for more effective proofreading. Auditory, visual, and tactile learners are given specific hints on ways to use their particular learning style to become better proofreaders.

The Proofreading Checklist

The checklist (p. 82) provides students with a useful guide to check their own writing errors. This tool may help students transfer the skills they've learned in *Find the Errors!* to their own writing projects.

To the Student

- Your teacher reads your essay. Finding several careless errors, he marks you down one full grade.

- A potential client reads the business letter you've sent, notices several errors, and decides that you don't sound very professional. He takes his business elsewhere.

- An employment interviewer reads the note you sent to thank her for the job interview. She is impressed with your manners. But she notices several mistakes in the note and wonders if she should hire someone else.

You can avoid embarrassing moments like these by proofreading everything you write. Look for mistakes in grammar, punctuation, and spelling. Careful, thorough proofreading of your work can be advantageous in several ways. Eliminating errors may improve your grades. On the job, you will have better opportunities for promotion and advancement. Sending well-written thank-you notes makes you shine on social occasions.

Most errors in writing are made because of inattention or carelessness. By getting the proofreading habit, you can quickly improve your writing. *Find the Errors!* reviews the "tools of writing" (including capitalization, punctuation, usage, sentence structure, and style), while giving you the opportunity to hone your proofreading skills.

Name _____ Date _____

Using Your Learning Style for Better Proofreading

- Tamika learns best when she can read the information she's studying over and over. She remembers things she sees better than information she hears. Tamika is a **visual** learner.

- Jeff learns best by hearing information. Reading aloud or listening to others talk helps him learn. Jeff is an **auditory** learner.

- Juan learns best by doing something active. Writing things down is helpful to him. Following the words he's reading with his finger helps him concentrate. Juan is a **tactile** learner.

- Which style of learner are you?

No matter which style of learning suits you best, you can use it to help you be a better proofreader! Here's how:

1. If you are primarily a visual learner, make it a practice to **scan slowly** everything you've written. If it's a very important piece of work, such as a job application, **read it over twice.** Look at each word and be sure it's right!

2. If you are an auditory learner, try **reading your written work aloud** as you proofread. Reading aloud will help you focus your attention on your writing. Mistakes will jump into focus when you hear your work.

3. If you are a tactile learner, try **moving your finger under the words** as you read them. Again, this will help you focus your attention on each word.

Of course, any or all of these ideas may be helpful to you! Try using one or more of these techniques for proofreading your work. See what works for you.

When you find a technique that's helpful, make it a habit. Proofread all your written work using the technique that works best for you. You'll find you have better luck finding your errors before someone else does! Eliminating careless mistakes from your written work can bring rewards at school, on the job, and in social situations. The proofreading habit is a habit worth developing.

viii   *Find the Errors!*

Find the Errors! Pretest

Background Information

This exercise is a pretest of the proofreading/writing skills presented in *Find the Errors!* The pretest may be used to determine specific areas in which students have difficulty. In addition, it may be used in conjunction with the posttest as an evaluation tool.

Each of the sentences in the pretest exemplifies one or more major writing errors. In the Answer Key below, each writing error has been correlated with the exercises that deal with that topic.

Answer Key

Pretest Sentence No.	Type of Error	Student Exercise No.
1–3	Capitalization	1–4, 34–36
4–11	Punctuation	5–13, 34–36
12	Misplaced or dangling modifiers	17–21, 35, 36
13	Subject/verb agreement	14, 19–21, 35, 36
14	Verb usage	15, 19, 35, 36
15	Pronoun usage	16, 19–21, 35, 36
16	Sentence fragment	22, 24, 25, 30–34, 35–36
17	Run-on sentences	23–25, 30–33, 35, 36
18	Tense consistency	26, 30–33, 35, 36
19	Lively vocabulary	27, 30–33, 35, 36

Pretest Sentence No.	Type of Error	Student Exercise No.
20	Wordiness	28, 30–33, 35, 36
21	Clichés	29, 30–33, 35, 36

The 10 misspelled words have been underlined and respelled correctly. They are *Mississippi*, *accompanied*, *principal*, *certified*, *beverages*, *it's*, *truly*, *athlete*, *attitude*, and *occasion*.

1. My father visited John Grisham, author of the novel A Time to Kill, in Oxford, Mississippi.

2. Our American history class visited the Museum of the Native American last month accompanied by Principal Thomas.

3. There are many Spanish-speaking Americans living in the western United States.

4. Did you give the certified letter to Mauricio C. Alegria, Ph.D.?

5. Dr. Alegria won $50,000 in the Publishers Clearinghouse contest.

6. Jens said, "Kandra, the party will be on Friday, May 17, at 392 High Street, Canton, New York."

7. Mykesia, our waitress, said, "The choice of beverages includes iced tea, soft drinks, and milk."

8. That was a long, tough test, but at least it's over.

9. The letter was signed, "Yours truly, Dr. M. L. King, Jr."

10. A two-thirds majority voted to ask the ex-athlete with the never-say-die attitude to speak at the occasion.

11. At 7:00 P.M. I'm meeting my three best friends: Avery, Latonya, and Melvin.

12. <u>After</u> <u>I</u> <u>escaped</u> from the car, the engine caught fire. (Answers will vary. Accept any reasonable answer.)

13. Every boy and girl in the seventh grade <u>is</u> invited.

14. Maggie <u>laid</u> the book on the bedside table, <u>set</u> her glasses on top of it, and then <u>lay</u> down to take a nap.

15. Free tickets were given to Mark and <u>me</u>.

16. A wonderful graduation party <u>was</u> <u>planned</u> for the entire class, all 150 of them. (Answers will vary. Accept any reasonable answer.)

17. Elmer slumped down in his seat<u>;</u> his worst fear was realized. OR: Elmer slumped down in his seat<u>.</u> <u>H</u>is worst fear was realized. OR: Elmer slumped down in his seat<u>,</u> his worst fear realized.

18. Helen passed the ball and then <u>rushed</u> down the field. OR: Helen <u>passes</u> the ball and then rushes down the field.

19. *The Grapes of Wrath* is a <u>very</u> <u>moving</u> book. (Students may use any word that is more specific than "nice.")

20. <u>I</u> <u>think</u> Skip is right<u>:</u> Spencer <u>does</u> <u>no</u> work. (Answers will vary. There are several acceptable alternatives. Students should eliminate either "in my opinion" or "I think." The phrase "in his thinking" is redundant. The phrase "never does no" is a double negative and should be changed to "does no" or "never works" or "never does his work.")

21. Passing that test was easy unless you work too slowly. (Students should eliminate the trite expressions "as easy as falling off a log" and "slow as molasses in January.")

Exercise I
Find the Errors! Pretest

Directions: Each sentence below has one or more major errors. The errors may be in capitalization, punctuation, or verb usage. You may find sentence fragments, run-on sentences, wordy sentences, clichés, or inconsistent verb tenses. There may be misplaced or dangling modifiers or incorrect pronouns.

Rewrite each sentence correctly in the space below it. There are also 10 misspelled words in this test. Circle each of the 10 words and rewrite them correctly as you rewrite the sentences. (Missing capital letters do not count as spelling errors.)

1. My father visited john grisham, author of the novel a time to kill, in oxford, missisippi.

2. Our american history class visited the museum of the native american last month, accompanyed by principle thomas.

3. There are many spanish-speaking americans living in the western United States.

4. Did you give the certifyed letter to Mauricio C Alegria PhD?

5. Dr Alegria won $50000 in the Publishers Clearinghouse contest.

(continued)

Exercise I
Find the Errors! Pretest *(continued)*

6. Jens said, "Kandra the party will be on Friday May 17 at 392 High Street Canton New York."

7. Mykesia our waitress said "The choice of bevrages includes iced tea soft drinks and milk."

8. That was a long tough test but at least its over.

9. The letter was signed, "Yours truely Dr M L King Jr."

10. A two thirds majority voted to ask the ex athelete with the never say die atitude to speak at the ocasion.

11. At 7 00 PM I'm meeting my three best friends Avery Latonya and Melvin.

12. Escaping from the car, the engine caught fire.

(continued)

Find the Errors!

Exercise I
Find the Errors! Pretest *(continued)*

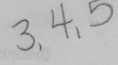

13. Every boy and girl in the seventh grade are invited.

14. Maggie lay the book on the bedside table, sat her glasses on top of it, and then laid down to take a nap.

15. Free tickets were given to Mark and I.

16. A wonderful graduation party for the entire class, all 150 of them.

17. Elmer slumped down in his seat, his worst fear was realized.

18. Helen passed the ball and then rushes down the field.

19. *The Grapes of Wrath* is a nice book.

20. In my opinion, I think Skip is right in his thinking that Spencer never does no work.

21. Passing that test was as easy as falling off a log unless you are as slow as molasses in January.

Find the Errors!

1. Let's Be Proper!

Background Information

This exercise deals with the capitalization of proper nouns and adjectives according to the following rules:

Rule 1: Capitalize all proper nouns. A proper noun names a particular person, place, or thing. (A common noun names one of a group of persons, places, or things and is not capitalized.)

Rule 2: Capitalize common nouns used as part of a proper noun. For example, in the proper noun *Casey Elementary School,* the word *school* should be capitalized since it is part of the proper noun.

Rule 3: Do not capitalize prepositions, the word *and,* or the articles *a, an,* or *the* when used as part of a proper noun (for example, *the* Statue of Liberty).

Answer Key

The story in Exercise 1 has been rewritten below with all proper nouns and adjectives capitalized and underlined. The misspelled words have been underlined and respelled correctly. They are *threw, know, especially, proceeded,* and *actually.*

Sir Arthur Conan Doyle was the author of the famous Sherlock Holmes stories. As you'll remember, Sherlock Holmes was the detective who could solve the most baffling case with only the remotest of clues.

One day Sir Arthur Conan Doyle hailed a cab in Paris. He threw in his small Samsonite suitcase and climbed into the cab.

The driver, a senior at the Sorbonne University, said, "Where to, Mr. Conan Doyle?"

"How do you know my name?" asked the author in surprise.

"Well, sir, I am a member of the Detective Fan Club. Yesterday I read in the *Paris Times* that you had been on vacation in a city in the south of France and were planning a visit to Paris in April. It is now April 1, or April Fool's Day, which should be a national holiday, in my opinion. I picked you up at the railroad station, where I observed you getting off the *Orient Express* train from the southern town of Marseilles. You have a nice tan, especially for so early in the spring. You look British. The royal blue ink stains on your fingers indicate you could be a writer. You are not speaking French. Putting all the clues together, I deduced that you could be none other than Sir Arthur Conan Doyle."

"That is remarkable work!" replied Doyle. "You yourself should be a detective with your keen powers of observation."

"Well," said the driver as they proceeded past the Eiffel Tower, "actually there is one other bit of supporting evidence I did not mention."

"And what is that?"

"There was also the fact that your name is written on your suitcase!"

Additional Activities

1. Write a list of common nouns on the board. Have students write two proper nouns for each one.

   Examples:

country	England	Somalia
park	Hyde Park	Yellowstone Park

2. Have students write a one-page paper describing their hometown. They should list its location, points of interest, major industries, schools, etc. Remind students to capitalize all proper nouns.

3. Write on the board pairs of words that could be either a proper noun or a common noun. Have students use each word you list in a sentence.

1. Let's Be Proper!

Directions: The story below has many proper nouns and adjectives that should be capitalized. Write in the capital letters where they are needed. Circle the five misspelled words in the story. Rewrite each word correctly in the Spelling Box.

sir arthur conan doyle was the author of the famous sherlock holmes stories. As you'll remember, sherlock holmes was the detective who could solve the most baffling case with only the remotest of clues.

One day sir arthur conan doyle hailed a cab in paris. He through in his small samsonite suitcase and climbed into the cab.

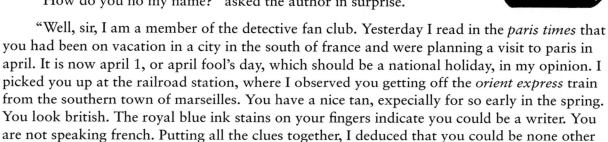

The driver, a senior at the sorbonne university, said, "Where to, mr. conan doyle?"

"How do you no my name?" asked the author in surprise.

"Well, sir, I am a member of the detective fan club. Yesterday I read in the *paris times* that you had been on vacation in a city in the south of france and were planning a visit to paris in april. It is now april 1, or april fool's day, which should be a national holiday, in my opinion. I picked you up at the railroad station, where I observed you getting off the *orient express* train from the southern town of marseilles. You have a nice tan, expecially for so early in the spring. You look british. The royal blue ink stains on your fingers indicate you could be a writer. You are not speaking french. Putting all the clues together, I deduced that you could be none other than sir arthur conan doyle."

"That is remarkable work!" replied doyle. "You yourself should be a detective with your keen powers of observation."

"Well," said the driver as they proceded past the eiffel tower, "actualy, there is one other bit of supporting evidence I did not mention."

"And what is that?"

"There was also the fact that your name is written on your suitcase!"

SPELLING BOX	1. _____	2. _____
3. _____	4. _____	5. _____

2. What a Capital Idea!
3. Another Capital Idea!

Background Information

Exercises 2 and 3 deal with correct use of capitalization, including the proper-noun rule (Exercise 1). Rules of capitalization used for these exercises include the following:

Rule 1: Capitalize the first word of a sentence.

Rule 2: Capitalize the first word of a quotation.

(*Example:* Ellen said, "*Everyone must go.*")

Rule 3: Capitalize titles and initials which are used as part of a person's name.

(*Example:* Principal *A. J.* Wilson)

Rule 4: Capitalize the word *I* and its contractions.

Rule 5: Capitalize the words *Mother, Father, Grandmother,* etc., if they are used as a person's name. Do not capitalize them if they are used in phrases such as "my mother."

Rule 6: Capitalize the first word and all important words in titles of books, plays, articles, paintings, periodicals, movies, musical compositions, poems, and other works of art. Capitalize small words like *a, an, the, in, on,* etc., only if they begin or end the title.

(*Example: The Old Man and the Sea* [book])

Rule 7: Capitalize the name of a school subject if it comes from the name of a country. Capitalize the name of a course followed by a Roman numeral. Do not capitalize other subjects.

(*Examples:* French, English, American History I, history, geography, algebra, etc.)

Rule 8: Capitalize direction words if they indicate a part of the country. Do not capitalize them if they merely indicate a direction.

(*Example:* They vacationed in the West. They drove west to Denver.)

Rule 9: Capitalize references to religions, denominations, the Bible, books of the Bible, or the Deity.

Rule 10: Capitalize all proper nouns and adjectives. (See the rules given for Exercise 1.)

Answer Key for Exercise 2

The story has been rewritten with correct capitalization. The misspelled words have been underlined and respelled correctly. They are *sophomores, distance, decided, answered,* and *whose.*

Two boys, Ali O. Wambari and Jacob P. Rust, were both sophomores at Hanging Moss High School. The two high school students were out for a Saturday drive in their Ford truck one day in August. They drove west from their hometown of Nanton some distance into a remote section of the West. They stopped in the small town of Mountain View to get something to eat at the town's only café, The Greasy Bucket Inn.

About that time, Ali noticed that his Timex watch had stopped. He decided to ask a man lounging in front of the café what time it was.

"I wonder if you could please tell me the time, sir?" Ali asked.

Just then, the bells of the nearby First Methodist Church began to ring.

"Well, the church bells say it's 12:00," answered the man, whose slow manner indicated he might not have made it past second grade.

"Oh, really?" replied the boy. "I'm so hungry I thought it must be much more than that!"

"Well, son, I don't have a lot of education. I never studied history, English or algebra. And I don't know much about those big cities like Big Timber. But around here it just goes up to 12:00 and then starts all over again!"

Answer Key for Exercise 3

The misspelled words are *skies, eighth, ninth, smiling,* and *stepped.*

The school band of Rockvale Junior High School was giving its annual fall concert. It was a pleasant October evening. A west wind was blowing gently, and the skies were clear. Clearly visible in the sky overhead were the Big Dipper, the Little Dipper, and the North Star. Indeed, it was a perfect setting for the open-air concert, which was entitled "Harvest Moon Concert."

The bandleader, Dr. Nolan C. Disharoon, had decided upon a variety of musical numbers to please his audience. The program ranged from classical music, such as the "William Tell Overture," to several popular rock numbers. The school band was made up of seventh, eighth, and ninth graders, including many students who were taking band for their first semester.

At the conclusion of one enthusiastic, if not overly harmonious, number, the audience (made up mostly of mothers and fathers) dutifully applauded the smiling musicians. Then the bandleader stepped to the podium and announced to the crowd, "For a change of pace after that beautiful slow piece, our next number will be the famous lively march 'Semper Fidelis.'"

Upon hearing this, the trumpet player turned to his friend and said, "Oh, no! I just got through playing that!"

Additional Activities

1. Have each student choose one rule for capitalization to illustrate and explain on a poster. Use your English grammar text to compile a list of rules to be illustrated. Encourage humor and creativity on the posters.

2. Have a student write a sentence on the board omitting all capital letters, and then call on another student to capitalize it correctly. Encourage students to make their sentences challenging to capitalize correctly.

3. Have students write an announcement about an upcoming event, either real or imaginary. The announcement should include the name of the event, the date, time, location, etc. Students may exchange announcements and then check for correct capitalization.

4. Have students write a letter to a class-mate describing a movie or book they enjoyed or an event they attended. Have students exchange letters and check for correct capitalization.

5. Many Native American words have become part of the English language. These include both common and proper nouns—for example, *chipmunk, squash, raccoon, muskrat, hickory, pecan, Chicago, Miami, teepee, pueblo, Mississippi,* and *moccasin.* Divide the class into teams. See which team can find the most common and proper nouns with a Native American origin.

6. Have students imagine they are present at a conversation between Dr. Martin Luther King and teens from their school. The group is discussing specific problems in your town and their possible solutions. Report on this conversation, using correct capitalization.

Name _____ Date _____

2. What a Capital Idea!

Directions: The story below contains many words that should be capitalized. Write in the capital letters where they are needed. Circle the five misspelled words in the story. Write each word correctly in the Spelling Box.

two boys, ali o. wambari and jacob p. rust, were both sophmores at hanging moss high school. the two high school students were out for a saturday drive in their ford truck one day in august. they drove west from their hometown of nanton some distence into a remote section of the west. they stopped in the small town of mountain view to get something to eat at the town's only café, the greasy bucket inn.

about that time, ali noticed that his timex watch had stopped. he desided to ask a man lounging in front of the café what time it was.

"i wonder if you could please tell me the time, sir?" ali asked.

just then, the bells of the nearby first methodist church began to ring.

"well, the church bells say it's 12:00," ansered the man, who's slow manner indicated he might not have made it past second grade.

"oh, really?" replied the boy. "i'm so hungry i thought it must be much more than that!"

"well, son, i don't have a lot of education. i never studied history, english or algebra. and i don't know much about those big cities like big timber. but around here it just goes up to 12:00 and then starts all over again!"

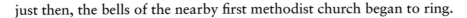

SPELLING BOX	1. _____	2. _____
3. _____	4. _____	5. _____

3. Another Capital Idea!

Directions: The story below contains many words that should be capitalized. Write in capital letters where they belong. Circle the five misspelled words. Rewrite each word correctly in the Spelling Box under the story.

the school band of rockvale junior high school was giving its annual fall concert. it was a pleasant october evening. a west wind was blowing gently, and the skys were clear. clearly visible in the sky overhead were the big dipper, the little dipper, and the north star. indeed, it was a perfect setting for the open-air band concert, which was entitled "harvest moon concert."

the bandleader, dr. nolan c. disharoon, had decided upon a variety of musical numbers to please his audience. the program ranged from classical music, such as the "william tell overture," to several popular rock numbers. the school band was made up of seventh, eigth, and nineth graders, including many students who were taking band for their first semester.

at the conclusion of one enthusiastic, if not overly harmonious, number, the audience (made up mostly of mothers and fathers) dutifully applauded the smileing musicians. then the bandleader steped to the podium and announced to the crowd, "for a change of pace after that beautiful slow piece, our next number will be the famous lively march 'semper fidelis.'"

upon hearing this, the trumpet player turned to his friend and said, "oh, no! i just got through playing that!"

SPELLING BOX	1. _____	2. _____
3. _____	4. _____	5. _____

4. Capital Letter Practice

Background Information

Exercise 4 is a review of the concepts presented in Exercises 1, 2, and 3.

Answer Key

The misspelled words are: *said, different, steelworkers, management,* and *college.*

<u>A</u> man was running for senator from a populous eastern state. <u>S</u>ince he was relatively unknown outside his own county, his campaign required that he and his wife travel north, south, east, and west to every corner of the state.

<u>O</u>ne evening in <u>S</u>eptember, the candidate's wife collapsed into a chair in the <u>C</u>hilton <u>H</u>otel, where they were staying. <u>S</u>he kicked off her expensive shoes and <u>said</u>, "<u>W</u>hat a day! <u>I</u> don't think <u>I</u>'ve ever been this tired!"

"<u>W</u>ell, <u>I</u> don't know why you should be tired," complained the husband. "<u>W</u>hat about me? <u>I</u> had to make seven <u>different</u> speeches today! <u>F</u>irst, <u>I</u> tried to convince the <u>steelworkers</u>' union that I was on their side and not with the steel company executives. <u>N</u>ext, <u>I</u> gave a rousing speech to the steel company executive board citing my longtime support of <u>management</u>.

"<u>I</u> spoke to a group of unemployed workers, outlining my early life of poverty. <u>T</u>hen <u>I</u> spoke at the <u>R</u>iverside <u>C</u>ountry <u>C</u>lub, emphasizing my aristocratic lineage, which my mother has traced back to sixteenth-century <u>E</u>ngland.

"<u>F</u>inally, <u>I</u> spoke at the <u>F</u>riends of the <u>L</u>ibrary <u>C</u>lub, where I recited the poem '<u>T</u>he <u>C</u>harge of the <u>L</u>ight <u>B</u>rigade.' After that there were speeches at a <u>college</u> and a law school. <u>S</u>o, why should *you* be tired? <u>Y</u>ou didn't have to do any of that!"

"<u>N</u>o, dear, <u>I</u> didn't," agreed his long-suffering wife. "<u>B</u>ut remember, I had to listen to you!"

Additional Activities

For additional review activities, see the teacher guide pages preceding Exercises 2 and 3.

4. Capital Letter Practice

Directions: The story below contains many capitalization errors. Write in capital letters where they are needed. Circle the five misspelled words. Rewrite each word correctly in the Spelling Box.

a man was running for senator from a populous eastern state. since he was relatively unknown outside his own county, his campaign required that he and his wife travel north, south, east, and west to every corner of the state.

one evening in september, the candidate's wife collapsed into a chair in the chilton hotel, where they were staying. she kicked off her expensive shoes and sayed, "what a day! i don't think i've ever been this tired!"

"well, i don't know why you should be tired," complained the husband. "what about me? i had to make seven diffrent speeches today! first, i tried to convince the steal-workers' union that i was on their side and not with the steel company executives. next, i gave a rousing speech to the steel company executive board citing my longtime support of managment.

"i spoke to a group of unemployed workers, outlining my early life of poverty. then i spoke at the riverside country club, emphasizing my aristocratic lineage, which my mother has traced back to sixteenth-century england.

"finally, i spoke at the friends of the library club, where i recited the poem 'the charge of the light brigade.' after that, there were speeches at a collige and a law school. so, why should *you* be tired? you didn't have to do any of that!"

"no, dear, i didn't," agreed his long-suffering wife. "but remember, i had to listen to you!"

SPELLING BOX	1. _____	2. _____
3. _____	4. _____	5. _____

5. Put an End to That!

Background Information

Exercise 5 includes practice on correct end punctuation, including periods, question marks, and exclamation points. It also includes other uses of the period.

Exclamatory sentences have been clearly identified as such by the use of such phrases as "exclaimed," "she shouted," and so on.

Rule 1: A statement (declarative sentence) is followed by a period.

Rule 2: Use a period at the end of an imperative sentence—that is, a command or a request.

Rule 3: A question (interrogative sentence) is followed by a question mark.

Rule 4: Use an exclamation point after an exclamation—that is, words that express strong feeling.

Rule 5: Use periods after abbreviations and after initials that stand for someone's name. (*Examples:* Mrs., Oct., and Bill J. Long)

Rule 6: Use a period with numerals to show dollars and cents.

Answer Key

Exercise 5 has been rewritten correctly below. Each punctuation mark the students should have added has been underlined. The misspelled words are underlined and rewritten correctly. The misspelled words are *Principal, speech, sitting, stare,* and *exclaimed.*

At a school function, Principal W. C. Sorey began a long, boring speech at 7:00 P.M. He began by telling the life story of the founder of Chastain Middle School, James C. Chastain. He hoped to inspire students to model their lives on this influential man.

Next, Mr. Sorey talked at length about how Chastain had improved since he had become principal. He listed all the new courses now available, including state history, Latin,

American studies, and computer literacy. A computer lab with computers from XYZ Corp. had been added. Also, six new teachers had been hired. Finally, a recent visit by the school superintendent and the governor had been highly successful.

By 8:30 P.M. a student, who had listened to the oration with increasing discomfort, turned to the lady sitting next to him.

"What a windbag he is!" he exclaimed. "Do you know that I will have been a student here for three years come Oct., and he's never yet said anything worth listening to? His remarks aren't worth $.02!" he added with feeling.

The lady turned to him with an icy stare. "Hush, young man! Do you know who I am?"

The student replied that he did not.

"I am the wife of that old windbag!" Mrs. Sorey shouted.

"You are?" asked the student. "And do you know who I am?"

The principal's wife said that she did not.

"Thank goodness!" exclaimed the student. He then turned and quickly left the room.

Additional Activities

1. Have students make up an advertising sign in which they use each (or as many as possible) of the rules listed under "Background Information" for Exercise 5.

2. Have students write and correctly punctuate original declarative, imperative, interrogative, and exclamatory sentences.

3. Have students work in teams. The first student is to write a sentence, leaving out the end punctuation. The second student is to punctuate the sentence correctly.

Name _____ Date _____

5. Put an End to That!

Directions: Add periods, question marks, and exclamation points wherever they are needed in the story below. Circle the five misspelled words. Rewrite each word correctly in the Spelling Box.

At a school function, Principle W C Sorey began a long, boring speach at 7:00 P M He began by telling the life story of the founder of Chastain Middle School, James C Chastain He hoped to inspire students to model their lives on this influential man

Next, Mr Sorey talked at length about how Chastain Middle School had improved since he had become principle He listed all the new courses now available, including state history, Latin, American studies, and computer literacy A computer lab with computers from XYZ Corp had been added Also, six new teachers had been hired Finally, a recent visit by the school superintendent and the governor had been highly successful

By 8:30 P M a student, who had listened to the oration with increasing discomfort, turned to the lady siting next to him

"What a windbag he is " he exclaimed "Do you know that I will have been a student here for three years come Oct , and he's never yet said anything worth listening to His remarks aren't worth $ 02 " he added with feeling.

The lady turned to him with an icy stair "Hush, young man Do you know who I am "

The student replied that he did not

"I am the wife of that old windbag " Mrs Sorey shouted

"You are " asked the student "And do you know who I am "

The principal's wife said that she did not

"Thank goodness " exclamed the student He then turned and quickly left the room

SPELLING BOX	1. _____	2. _____
3. _____	4. _____	5. _____

6. Time for a Break!
7. More Break Time!

Background Information

Exercises 6 and 7 deal with the correct use of commas. Students will need to add commas to the stories in Exercises 6 and 7 according to the following rules.

Rule 1: Use commas after the parts of an address.

(*Example:* He lives at 422 Meadow Road, Jackson, MS.)

Rule 2: Use commas after parts of a date.

(*Example:* Saturday, October 1, 1893)

Rule 3: Use a comma or commas to set off a noun in direct address.

(*Example:* "Hey, John, where are you going?" he shouted.)

Rule 4: Use a comma or commas to set off appositives.

(*Example:* Dr. Smith, the author, is our neighbor.)

Rule 5: Use commas to separate three or more items in a series. (Publishers differ as to the use of a comma before the *and* joining the last two items in a series. Instruct your students which practice you prefer. In *Find the Errors!* the comma before the *and* has been included.)

(*Example:* You can choose among pizza, hamburgers, and hot dogs.)

Rule 6: Use a comma after an introductory word like *yes, no, well,* or *oh.*

(*Example:* Well, I'll think about it.)

Rule 7: Use a comma or commas to separate a quotation from the rest of the sentence.

(*Example:* "I'll go," said Jack, "if you want me to.")

Rule 8: Use a comma to separate two or more adjectives preceding a noun.

(*Example:* That was a long, tough, challenging test.)

Rule 9: Use a comma to separate two independent clauses joined by *and, but, or, nor, for,* or *yet.*

(*Example:* We went swimming in the lake, and we had a hamburger cookout.)

Rule 10: Use a comma to set off nonessential clauses and nonessential participial phrases.

(*Example:* My neighbor, who loves animals, has three cats and three dogs.)

Rule 11: Use a comma after an introductory participial phrase, a series of introductory prepositional phrases, or an introductory adverb clause.

(*Examples:* Awakened by the noise, the baby began to cry. Near the tree at the end of the yard, the children built a playhouse. After Bill had presented his piano recital, the audience applauded loudly.)

Rule 12: Use a comma after the salutation of a friendly letter and after the closing of any letter.

Rule 13: Use a comma after a name followed by *Jr., Sr.,* or *M.D.*

(*Example:* John Jones, M.D.)

Rule 14: Parenthetical expressions are set off by commas.

(*Example:* He did, of course, pass the test.)

Rule 15: Avoid using any unnecessary commas.

Answer Key for Exercise 6

The misspelled words have been underlined and rewritten correctly. They are *tomorrow, vacuum, wastebasket, potatoes,* and *gratefully.*

"Dad, I need some help with my homework, and I was wondering if you have time to help me out. I have work in several subjects, and all of it is due <u>tomorrow</u>," Elena stated.

"Of course, dear. Tell me the first question, and I'll give it my best shot," Dad replied.

"Well, for English we have to list some collective nouns," Elena said.

"That's easy! Vacuum cleaner, wastebasket, and garbage truck!" answered Dad.

"Next, I need to define the word *synonym*," Elena said, writing furiously.

"A synonym is a word you use when you don't know how to spell the other word," Dad answered.

Elena continued, "Great, Dad, now for math. You have 4 potatoes to divide evenly among 3 people. How much would each person get?"

"Just mash the potatoes, and then you can give each person the same size scoop," Dad suggested.

"I'm sorry that this is getting to be a long, boring list of questions, but now we'll move on to American history. First question: Where was the Declaration of Independence signed?"

"At the bottom, of course," Dad said quickly.

"We're almost through, Dad," Elena said, "but next I need to know what the Declaration of Independence is."

"A note excusing you from school!" Dad replied.

"I hope you didn't mind so many questions, did you?" Elena asked gratefully.

"Of course not, Elena. How else are you going to become educated?" Dad answered with a smile.

Answer Key for Exercise 7

Exercise 7 has been rewritten correctly. Each comma the students should have added has been underlined. The misspelled words have been underlined and rewritten correctly. They are *metal, angle, its, calculator,* and *amazement.*

Mr. O'Brian was walking down the street in Jackson, Arizona. He really needed to know the time, but he had forgotten to put on his watch that morning. Seeing an old man

sitting on his front porch, Mr. O'Brian stopped and asked, "Sir, do you by any chance have the time?"

"Ah, the time. One moment, son." Leaping up from his rocking chair, the old man took a metal rod and a hammer. Tapping the metal rod into the ground, he adjusted it and measured it with his protractor until it formed an exact 90° angle with the ground. He then pulled out a measuring tape, and he measured the length of the metal rod and its shadow. Stretching out on the ground, he sighted the top of the rod with a point on a nearby tree. Then he made a mark on the ground and some additional measurements. Pulling his calculator out of his pocket, he punched the buttons in silence.

Finally, he announced, "I have it! It is Friday, August 15, 1998, and it is exactly 10:32 A.M.!"

Mr. O'Brian, who had been watching all this in amazement, said to the old man, "Well, you really know how to tell time by using the sun. But what do you do if it's cloudy, as it often is around here, or at night? Then you would have no shadows to measure, would you?"

"Oh," said the old fellow, holding up his arm, "in that case, I just look at my watch!"

Additional Activities

1. Have students make up an advertising sign in which they use each (or as many as possible) of the rules listed under "Background Information" for Exercise 6.

2. Have students write and correctly punctuate original declarative, imperative, interrogative, and exclamatory sentences, including as many commas as possible.

3. Have students work in teams. The first student is to write a sentence, leaving out any punctuation. The second student is to punctuate the sentence correctly.

6. Time for a Break!

Directions: Add commas wherever they are needed in the conversation below. Circle the five misspelled words in the story. Rewrite each word correctly in the Spelling Box.

"Dad I need some help with my homework and I was wondering if you have time to help me out. I have work in several subjects and all of it is due tommorow " Elena stated.

"Of course dear. Tell me the first question and I'll give it my best shot " Dad replied.

"Well for English we have to list some collective nouns " Elena said.

"That's easy! Vaccum cleaner waistbasket and garbage truck!" answered Dad.

"Next I need to define the word *synonym* " Elena said writing furiously.

"A synonym is a word you use when you don't know how to spell the other word " Dad answered.

Elena continued "Great Dad now for math. You have 4 potatos to divide evenly among 3 people. How much would each person get?"

"Just mash the potatoes and then you can give each person the same size scoop " Dad suggested.

"I'm sorry that this is getting to be a long boring list of questions but now we'll move on to American history. First question: Where was the Declaration of Independence signed?"

"At the bottom of course " Dad said quickly.

"We're almost through Dad " Elena said "but next I need to know what the Declaration of Independence is."

"A note excusing you from school!" Dad replied.

"I hope you didn't mind so many questions did you?" Elena asked greatfully.

"Of course not Elena. How else are you going to become educated?" Dad answered with a smile.

SPELLING BOX	1. _____	2. _____
3. _____	4. _____	5. _____

    18   *Find the Errors!*

7. More Break Time!

Directions: Add commas wherever they are needed in the story below. Circle the five misspelled words. Rewrite each word correctly in the Spelling Box.

Mr. O'Brian was walking down the street in Jackson Arizona. He really needed to know the time but he had forgotten to put on his watch that morning. Seeing an old man sitting on his front porch Mr. O'Brian stopped and asked "Sir do you by any chance have the time?"

"Ah the time. One moment son." Leaping up from his rocking chair the old man took a medal rod and a hammer. Tapping the metal rod into the ground he adjusted it and measured it with his protractor until it formed an exact 90° angel with the ground. He then pulled out a measuring tape and he measured the length of the metal rod and it's shadow. Stretching out on the ground he sighted the top of the rod with a point on a nearby tree. Then he made a mark on the ground and some additional measurements. Pulling his calculator out of his pocket he punched the buttons in silence.

Finally he announced "I have it! It is Friday August 15 1998 and it is exactly 10:32 A.M.!"

Mr. O'Brian who had been watching all this in amazment said to the old man "Well you really know how to tell time by using the sun. But what do you do if it's cloudy as it often is around here or at night? Then you would have no shadows to measure would you?"

"Oh " said the old fellow holding up his arm "in that case I just look at my watch!"

SPELLING BOX	1. _____	2. _____
3. _____	4. _____	5. _____

8. What Did He Say?

Background Information

Exercise 8 involves correct usage of quotation marks. The following rules are included:

Rule 1: Use quotation marks before and after a direct quotation.

(*Examples:* "I think that he went home," Bill said. "I think," said Bill, "that he went home.")

Rule 2: Do not use quotation marks for an indirect quotation.

(*Example:* Bill said that he thought Joe went home.)

Rule 3: In writing conversation, begin a new paragraph and use new quotation marks to indicate each change of speaker.

Rule 4: Use quotation marks around titles of short stories, one-act plays, articles, songs, poems, and themes.

Rule 5: Use single quotation marks to enclose a quotation within a quotation.

(*Example:* Mrs. Brown asked, "Why did you yell 'Help!'?")

Answer Key

The misspelled words are *tough, tried, it's, desperately,* and *communications.*

Last week, my older brother Nick, who is 19, came home on leave from the army. Since I hadn't seen him for three months, I was full of questions about army life.

"Hey, Nick," I asked, "how's army life?"

"Fine," he replied.

"I heard that basic training can be pretty tough," I said.

"Yeah," came the reply.

"Well," I tried again, "is army food as bad as they say it is?"

"Yep," he answered.

"I'll bet it's easy to get dates," I continued, "especially when you wear your uniform."

"It sure is!"

"Have you made any friends yet?" I asked.

"Yes."

"How's life in the barracks, then?"

"Good."

"Have you decided in what area you'll ask for special training?" I asked.

"Yes," he said.

"What is it?" I probed, somewhat desperately.

"Communications," he replied.

Additional Activities

1. Have students write three pairs of sentences illustrating direct and indirect quotations.

   Example:
   Harry said, "I'm ready."
   Harry said that he was ready.

2. Have students write a page of dialogue using quotation marks correctly. It could be an anecdote or a discussion from real life.

3. Have students imagine that they and a friend are planning an evening out. They are to write a dialogue in which they discuss their options. Caution students to use quotation marks correctly. This can be done in teams or individually.

4. Have students choose a magazine photograph that has two or more people in it. They are to make up a conversation the two people could be having. Write it down, punctuating correctly.

8. What Did He Say?

Directions: Add quotation marks and commas wherever they are needed to set off a direct quotation in the story below. Circle the five misspelled words. Rewrite each word correctly in the Spelling Box.

Last week, my older brother Nick, who is 19, came home on leave from the army. Since I hadn't seen him for three months, I was full of questions about army life.

Hey, Nick I asked how's army life?

Fine he replied.

I heard that basic training can be pretty tuff I said.

Yeah came the reply.

Well I tryed again is army food as bad as they say it is?

Yep he answered.

I'll bet its easy to get dates, I continued, especially when you wear your uniform.

It sure is!

Have you made any friends yet? I asked.

Yes.

How's life in the barracks, then?

Good.

Have you decided in what area you'll ask for special training? I asked.

Yes he said.

What is it? I probed, somewhat desparately.

Comunications he replied.

SPELLING BOX	1. _____	2. _____
3. _____	4. _____	5. _____

21   *Find the Errors!*

9. Some Troublemakers

Background Information

This exercise covers using colons, hyphens, and underlining or italicizing correctly according to the following rules:

Hyphens

Rule 1: Use a hyphen to divide a word between syllables at the end of a line.

Rule 2: Use a hyphen with compound numbers from twenty-one to ninety-nine. Use a hyphen with fractions used as adjectives.

(*Example:* a two-thirds majority)

Rule 3: Use a hyphen with prefixes such as *ex-, all-, self-,* etc.

(*Examples:* ex-player, all-star)

Rule 4: Use hyphens when using a compound adjective in front of a noun.

(*Example:* He has a never-say-die attitude.)

Colons

Rule 1: Use a colon when you write the time in numerals.

Rule 2: Use a colon before a list of items, especially after expressions like *as follows.*

(*Example:* I have three best friends: Joe, Bill, and Amy.)

Rule 3: Use a colon between chapter and verse of the Bible.

(*Example:* John 3:15)

Rule 4: Use a colon after the salutation of a business letter.

Rule 5: Use a colon before a long formal statement or quotation.

(*Example:* President Clinton had this to say on the subject of national security: "...")

Underlining or Italics

Rule 1: When you write or type, underline or italicize titles of books, magazines, newspapers, plays, long musical compositions, works of art, and ships.

Rule 2: Use underlining or italics for foreign words and for words, letters, and figures referred to as such.

(*Examples:* The word <u>success</u> is often misspelled. <u>Bonjour</u> means hello in French.)

Answer Key

The misspelled words are *enough, weight, dollars, cents,* and *column.*

1. <u>Boy's Life</u>   as follows<u>:</u>   enough   weight
2. <u>Jackson Times</u>   ex-convict
3. seventy<u>-</u>five<u>-</u>year<u>-</u>old watch
4. 5<u>:</u>30
5. <u>Camera Tricks</u>   cam-era (hyphenated at end of line)   this reason:
6. <u>Newsday</u>   ninety<u>-</u>five dollars   seventy<u>-</u>five cents   as follows<u>:</u>
7. this way<u>:</u>   ear<u>-</u>to<u>-</u>ear carpeting
8. <u>polygon</u>   wrote this<u>:</u>
9. <u>California Sun</u>   personal column<u>:</u>   Bach-elor (should be hyphenated at the end of line)   Object<u>:</u>

Additional Activities

1. Have students use a dictionary to review division of words into syllables.
2. Have students write 10 sentences in which they tell about their favorite books or magazines. Remind them to be careful to underline names of books and magazines.
3. Have students write paragraphs about their three favorite movies, explaining why they made their choices. Make sure underlining is used correctly.
4. Have students write a business letter in which they complain about the quality of a product. They are to use at least two colons and two hyphens in the letter. Remind students that a courteous letter will get better results than one that is rude.

9. Some Troublemakers

Directions: Add colons, hyphens, or underlining/italics wherever they are needed in the sentences below. Circle the five misspelled words. Rewrite each word correctly in the Spelling Box.

1. In the book Boy's Life, Sammy gave his reason for not cutting the grass as follows "If it gets long enuf it'll fall over from its own wait."

2. I read in the Jackson Times about the ex convict who ended up saving his neighbor's life.

3. My dad calls his seventy five year old watch an old timer.

4. Jerinda taught her dog to beg. At 5 30 P.M. last night it came home with $57.22.

5. According to the book Camera Tricks, scientists have developed a cam era that can take photographs of the entire world. They tried one, but the picture turned out terrible for this reason somebody moved!

6. Newsday magazine had a story about a panhandler who asked a man for ninety five dollers for a cup of coffee. The man protested that coffee only costs seventy five sense. The panhandler replied as follows "You certainly don't expect me to drink it in these old clothes, do you?"

7. One barber defines a toupee this way ear to ear carpeting.

8. Given the assignment to use the word polygon in a sentence, one student wrote this "My parrot, Polly, flew away. I wonder where polygon."

9. This ad was run in the California Sun newspaper's personal colum "Bach elor with income of $100,000 seeks woman with four or more children. Object marriage and instant tax deductions."

SPELLING BOX	1. _____	2. _____
3. _____	4. _____	5. _____

             Find the Errors!

10. The Versatile Apostrophe

Background Information

In Exercise 10, students need to add apostrophes according to the following rules:

Rule 1: Use apostrophes to show ownership.

(*Examples:* Mary's dress, my bride-to-be's gown, children's voices, the two boys' bicycles)

Rule 2: Use apostrophes to form contractions.

(*Examples:* I'll, don't)

Rule 3: Use an apostrophe and an *s* to form the plurals of figures, signs, letters, and words referred to as such.

(*Examples:* There are two 6's in our phone number.
How many *x*'s can you make in five seconds?
There are three *a*'s in *aardvark.*
Eliminate some of the *and*'s from your paragraph.)

Answer Key

The misspelled words are *catalog, running, competitors, shipping,* and *receipt.*

Ian Davis entered the <u>town's</u> largest sporting goods store with a mail-order <u>catalog</u> in hand. He searched the racks of <u>running</u> shoes until he found the exact pair <u>he'd</u> been wanting.

"<u>What's</u> the price on these shoes?" he asked the salesclerk.

"<u>Let's</u> see. <u>It's</u> either $53.05 or $58.05. <u>It's</u> hard to tell the difference between <u>3's</u> and <u>8's</u> on some of these price tags. Let me ask the manager," the salesclerk said politely. "<u>That's</u> what I thought," he continued after a <u>minute's</u> wait. "The price is $58.05!"

"But the shoes in this catalog are the same as yours, and <u>they're</u> selling for $49.95," Ian complained.

"<u>It's</u> store policy to match the prices of its <u>competitors</u>," the clerk replied. "But <u>you'd</u> have to pay $8.95 for <u>shipping</u> and handling if you ordered the shoes from the catalog. <u>That's</u> a total of $58.90."

"<u>That's</u> not much savings. <u>It's</u> only a difference of $.85," Ian figured. "Well, it all adds up," he laughed as he paid for the shoes at the lower price.

As Ian reached for the shoes, the <u>clerk's</u> smile broadened. Putting the shoes under the counter, he said, "<u>Here's</u> your <u>receipt</u>. You can come back and pick up the shoes in two weeks. <u>That's</u> how long <u>you'd</u> have waited for your mail-order shoes to arrive!"

Additional Activities

1. Write lists of singular and plural nouns on the board. Have students write each word's possessive form.

2. Obtain a list of contractions. Have students rewrite these as individual words.

3. Have students write a one-page conversation between two friends. In it, they should use at least 10 contractions and 5 possessives.

4. Have students write sentences containing plural figures, signs, letters, and words referred to as words.
    Example:
    On his typing test, he mistakenly typed three +'s, two *x*'s and four *R*'s.

5. Have each student write a note to a classmate in which at least 15 apostrophes are used correctly. Students may exchange notes and look for correct use of apostrophes.

6. Have students imagine that a famous African American, Hispanic American, Native American, or Asian American comes to speak to your class. Have students write what the visitor might say, using as many apostrophes as possible in their imaginary speeches.

10. The Versatile Apostrophe

Directions: Add apostrophes to the story below as needed. Circle the five misspelled words. Rewrite each word correctly in the Spelling Box.

Ian Davis entered the towns largest sporting goods store with a mail-order catelog in hand. He searched the racks of runing shoes until he found the exact pair hed been wanting.

"Whats the price on these shoes?" he asked the salesclerk.

"Lets see. Its either $53.05 or $58.05. Its hard to tell the difference between 3s and 8s on some of these price tags. Let me ask the manager," the salesclerk said politely. "Thats what I thought," he continued after a minutes wait. "The price is $58.05!"

"But the shoes in this catalog are the same as yours, and theyre selling for $49.95," Ian complained.

"Its store policy to match the prices of its competiters," the clerk replied. "But youd have to pay $8.95 for shiping and handling if you ordered the shoes from the catalog. Thats a total of $58.90."

"Thats not much savings. Its only a difference of $.85," Ian figured. "Well, it all adds up," he laughed as he paid for the shoes at the lower price.

As Ian reached for the shoes, the clerks smile broadened. Putting the shoes under the counter, he said, "Heres your reciept. You can come back and pick up the shoes in two weeks. Thats how long youd have waited for your mail-order shoes to arrive!"

SPELLING BOX	1. _____	2. _____
3. _____	4. _____	5. _____

11. Punctuation Practice
12. Practice Makes Perfect!
13. Review Time

Background Information

These three exercises provide a review of the concepts presented in Exercises 1–11.

(**Note:** Students may differ in their use of exclamation points. Explain that they should use exclamation points to indicate strong feeling. In some sentences the use of an exclamation point is clearly called for; in other sentences you will have to use your own judgment on whether or not the exclamation point is appropriate.)

Answer Key for Exercise 11

The stories in Exercise 11 have been rewritten below. Each punctuation mark and capital letter the students should have added has been underlined. The misspelled words are *doubt, nervously, replied, one,* and *appearing.*

1. The teacher said to his new pupil, "Well, young lady, I hope you understand the following point: correct punctuation is most important!"

    "Yes, sir!" the pupil exclaimed, "I always get to class on time!"

2. A teacher was upset at one pupil's poor spelling. "There is no ex-cuse for this poor spelling!" he shouted. "You should consult a dictionary whenever you're in doubt!"

    "But," replied the dazed student, "I'm never in doubt."

3. The young man said nervously to a girl he admired, "If you'll give me your phone number, I'll give you a call."

    She replied, "It's in the telephone book."

    "OK," he pursued, "but what's your name?"

    Enthusiastically, she replied, "Oh, that's in the phone book, too!"

4. "Mother," said the teenage girl, "what's the name of the boy I met on my vacation?"

    "Which one, dear?"

    "You know," she exclaimed, "the one I couldn't live without!"

5. A student strolled into class at 10:00 A.M., 30 minutes late. The teacher said, "You should have been here at 9:30."

    The pupil, appearing confused, exclaimed, "Why, what happened?"

Answer Key for Exercise 12

Exercise 12 is rewritten correctly below. The misspelled words are *borrowed, two, all right, library,* and *Saturday.*

Conner Jones, a freshman at Lake High School, was searching desperately through the stacks of the Billings Library for a book on ancient history which he had borrowed several weeks before on Veteran's Day. Two librarians, Mrs. Cole and Mr. Goldstein, joined in the search. Several hours passed. Row after row of books was examined carefully.

Finally, Mrs. Cole called out that she had located the book, Homer's Ancient History. It had mistakenly been shelved in the juvenile fiction area on the fourth floor instead of the adult nonfiction area on the first floor.

Panting from exertion, Mrs. Cole said, "Now then, let's take it to the circulation desk, and I'll check it out for you."

"No, thank you, Ma'am," Conner replied. "It'll only take me a minute to locate the information I need and copy it."

"All right, perhaps you'd like to find yourself a comfortable armchair in the Gates Memorial Reading Room," she continued.

"Thanks, but it's really not necessary. I only need a number off the inside front cover."

"Well," exclaimed the librarian, "I hope it's a pretty important number to keep us running all over the library all Saturday afternoon!"

"Oh, it is!" said Conner excitedly. "You see, I met this terrific girl, and that's her new unlisted phone number!"

Answer Key for Exercise 13

Exercise 13 is rewritten correctly below. The misspelled words are *a lot, interrupted, message, accelerator,* and *brake.*

Mr. Bowman was taking a long-awaited day off from his job at Hunter Construction Company. He had been putting in a lot of overtime, and he really needed some time to relax. His plans for the day included sleeping late, sunbathing, reading a good book, and taking a nap.

Not long after he woke up, his daughter Kelly asked, "Dad, will you please take me to Lindsey's house?" Mr. Bowman drove Kelly the four blocks to Lindsey's house, and then he prepared to stretch out with his book.

Settling down in his recliner, Mr. Bowman had five minutes to read before he was interrupted by his son Max. "Dad, will you take Isaac and me to the movie? Star Wars X is playing at the Alamo

Theater, and we don't want to miss it!" Max pleaded.

Good-naturedly, Mr. Bowman got up and took the boys the five blocks to the theater. Returning home, he decided to do a little sunbathing. After changing into his swimsuit, he stretched out in the sun. It was then that little Chris came out. "I need a ride to Grenada Field for baseball practice," he said.

Mr. Bowman drove Chris the three blocks to practice, and then he came home. Awaiting him on the answering machine was a message from Kelly. "Dad, please come pick me up at Lindsey's. I'm ready to come home." she said.

Once again, Mr. Bowman was in the car. Returning home and trying to read his book, he was soon interrupted by calls from Max and Chris. Both boys asked their father to pick them up.

At the dinner table that night, Mr. Bowman was telling his wife, Judy, about his day. Telling of the day's events, he began to feel sorry for himself. "I don't know what's the matter with kids today," he began. "They think they need to be driven everywhere! Don't you kids know what feet are for?"

"Of course, Dad," they all chorused. "The right foot is for the accelerator, and the left foot is for the brake!"

11. Punctuation Practice

Directions: Correctly punctuate the following anecdotes. You will need to add periods, question marks, exclamation points, commas, quotation marks, colons, underlining or italics, hyphens, and apostrophes. You will also need to add some capital letters. Circle the five misspelled words. Rewrite each word correctly in the Spelling Box.

1. The teacher said to his new pupil well young lady I hope you understand the following point correct punctuation is most important

   Yes sir the pupil exclaimed I always get to class on time

2. A teacher was upset at one pupils poor spelling There is no ex cuse for this poor spelling he shouted You should consult a dictionary whenever youre in dout

   But replied the dazed student Im never in doubt

3. The young man said nervusly to a girl he admired if youll give me your phone number Ill give you a call

   She replyed its in the telephone book

   OK he pursued but whats your name

   Enthusiastically she replied oh thats in the phone book too

4. Mother said the teenage girl whats the name of the boy I met on my vacation

   Which won dear

   You know she exclaimed the one I couldn't live without

5. A student strolled into class at 10:00 A.M. 30 minutes late.

   The teacher said you should have been here at 9:30.

   The pupil appeering confused exclaimed why what happened?

SPELLING BOX	1. _____	2. _____
3. _____	4. _____	5. _____

12. Practice Makes Perfect!

Directions: Add capital letters and punctuation as needed in the story below. Circle the five misspelled words. Rewrite each word correctly in the Spelling Box.

conner jones a freshman at lake high school was searching desperately through the stacks of the billings library for a book on ancient history which he had borowed several weeks before on veterans day too librarians mrs cole and mr goldstein joined in the search several hours passed row after row of books was examined carefully.

finally mrs cole called out that she had located the book homers ancient history it had mistakenly been shelved in the juvenile fiction area on the fourth floor instead of the adult nonfiction area on the first floor

panting from exertion mrs cole said now then lets take it to the circulation desk and ill check it out for you

no thank you ma am conner replied itll only take me a minute to locate the information i need and copy it

alright perhaps youd like to find yourself a comfortable armchair in the gates memorial reading room she continued

thanks but its really not necessary i only need a number off the inside front cover

well exclaimed the librarian i hope its a pretty important number to keep us running all over the libary all saterday afternoon

oh it is said conner excitedly you see i met this terrific girl and thats her new unlisted phone number

SPELLING BOX	1. _____	2. _____
3. _____	4. _____	5. _____

13. Review Time

Directions: Add capital letters and punctuation where needed in the story below. Circle the five misspelled words. Rewrite each word correctly in the Spelling Box.

mr bowman was taking a long awaited day off from his job at hunter construction company. He had been putting in alot of overtime and he really needed some time to relax. His plans for the day included sleeping late sunbathing reading a good book and taking a nap.

Not long after he woke up his daughter kelly asked dad will you please take me to lindsey s house? mr bowman drove kelly the four blocks to lindsey s house and then he prepared to stretch out with his book.

Settling down in his recliner mr bowman had five minutes to read before he was interupted by his son max. dad will you take isaac and me to the movie? Star Wars X is playing at the alamo theater and we don't want to miss it! max pleaded.

Good-naturedly mr bowman got up and took the boys the five blocks to the theater. Returning home, he decided to do a little sunbathing. After changing into his swimsuit he stretched out in the sun. It was then that little chris came out. I need a ride to grenada field for baseball practice he said.

mr bowman drove chris the three blocks to practice, and then he came home. Awaiting him on the answering machine was a messige from kelly. dad please come pick me up at lindsey s. I'm ready to come home she said.

Once again mr bowman was in the car. Returning home and trying to read his book he was soon interrupted by calls from max and chris. Both boys asked their father to pick them up.

At the dinner table that night, mr bowman was telling his wife judy about his day. Telling of the day's events he began to feel sorry for himself. I don't know what's the matter with kids today he began. They think they need to be driven everywhere! Don't you kids know what feet are for?

Of course dad they all chorused. The right foot is for the acelerator and the left foot is for the break!

SPELLING BOX	1. _____	2. _____
3. _____	4. _____	5. _____

14. Peaceful Coexistence

Background Information

Exercise 14 deals with agreement of subject and verb. The rules are as follows:

Rule 1: Use a singular verb with a singular subject.

Rule 2: Use a plural verb with a plural subject.

Rule 3: The number of the subject is not changed by a phrase following the subject.
(*Example:* This tree, unlike some others, grows quickly.)

Rule 4: These pronouns are singular: each, either, neither, one, everyone, everybody, no one, nobody, anyone, anybody, someone, and somebody.
(*Example:* Each of us *is* coming.)

Rule 5: These pronouns are plural: several, few, both, and many.
(*Example:* Several of us *are* coming.)

Rule 6: These pronouns may be either singular or plural: *some*, *all*, *most*, *any*, or *none*.
(*Examples:* Most of the play was interesting. Most of the plays we saw were interesting.)

Rule 7: Subjects joined by *and* take a plural verb.
(*Example:* Joe and Mary are coming to visit.)

Rule 8: Singular subjects joined by *or* or *nor* take singular verbs.
(*Example:* Joe or Mary is coming to visit.)

Rule 9: If a singular subject and a plural subject are joined by *or* or *nor* the verb agrees with the subject nearer the verb.
(*Example:* Two boys or one girl is still able to sign up.)

Rule 10: Words stating amounts are usually singular.
(*Example:* Twenty-five dollars is the entrance fee.)

Rule 11: *Every* or *many a* before a subject calls for a singular verb.
(*Example:* Many a songwriter starts in Nashville.)

Answer Key

Each verb in the story that was used incorrectly has been marked with an asterisk (*) and corrected. Each word that was spelled incorrectly has been underlined and respelled correctly. The misspelled words are *license, naturally, successfully, beginning,* and *relief.*

Jim is preparing for his driver's <u>license</u> exam. First, with the help of his two older brothers, Jim *practices driving the family car around town. Jim knows that the rules in the driver's handbook *need to be learned. Jim's driving handbook, unlike his other school books, *rates careful study every evening. <u>Naturally</u>, every one of Jim's friends wants to pass the exam, too. Even the most reluctant students *study hard for the driver's license exam.

Finally, the day for the written and driving tests arrives. A written test of the road rules starts the exam. Each question on driving and car use *is carefully and correctly answered. Jim scores 100 percent. The test for his eyes presents no problem for him either.

Then the actual driving section of the tests *begins. Jim completes each of the maneuvers <u>successfully</u>. In fact, Jim, unlike many of his friends, *has driven a nearly perfect exam. But Jim, like so many <u>beginning</u> drivers on the first try, does not get his license.

Jim makes his only mistake as he stops slowly and carefully to let his examiner out of the car. Breathing a sigh of <u>relief</u>, Jim exclaims, "Boy, I'm sure glad I don't have to drive like that all the time!"

Additional Activities

1. Write additional sentences on the board, making agreement errors in some and not in others. Include several sentences illustrating each rule on the teacher guide page. Have students decide if each sentence is correct or incorrect.

2. Have students write a paragraph about their favorite and least favorite foods using sentences with compound subjects. Be sure the subject and verb agree in each sentence.

3. Have students write a sentence to illustrate each of the 11 rules on subject-verb agreement listed on the teacher guide page.

4. Divide the class in half. Have one group of students write sentences with correct or incorrect subject-verb agreement on the board. Have the other team tell whether the sentence is correct. Keep score.

14. Peaceful Coexistence

Directions: The story below contains several errors in the agreement of subject and verb. Look carefully at each underlined verb in the story. If it is incorrect, cross it out and write the correct form of the verb above it. Circle the five misspelled words. Rewrite each word correctly in the Spelling Box.

Jim is preparing for his driver's lisence exam. First, with the help of his two older brothers, Jim <u>practice</u> driving the family car around town. Jim knows that the rules in the driver's handbook <u>needs</u> to be learned. Jim's driving handbook, unlike his other school books, <u>rate</u> careful study every evening. Naturaly, every one of Jim's friends <u>wants</u> to pass the exam, too. Even the most reluctant students <u>studies</u> hard for the driver's license exam.

Finally, the day for the written and driving tests <u>arrives</u>. A written test of the road rules <u>starts</u> the exam. Each question on driving and car use <u>are</u> carefully and correctly answered. Jim <u>scores</u> 100 percent. The test for his eyes <u>presents</u> no problem for him either.

Then the actual driving section of the tests <u>begin</u>. Jim completes each of the manuevers sucessfully. In fact, Jim, unlike many of his friends, <u>have</u> driven a nearly perfect exam. But Jim, like so many begining drivers on the first try, <u>does</u> not get his license.

Jim makes his only mistake as he stops slowly and carefully to let his examiner out of the car. Breathing a sigh of releif, Jim exclaims, "Boy, I'm sure glad I don't have to drive like that all the time!"

SPELLING BOX	1. _____	2. _____
3. _____	4. _____	5. _____

15. Principal Problems with Principal Parts

Background Information

This exercise provides practice choosing the correct principal part of a variety of verbs. Special emphasis is placed on verbs often confused, such as: *lie* and *lay,* *rise* and *raise,* and *sit* and *set.*

The principal part of these six verbs are as follows: lie (to rest or recline): lie, lying, lay, have lain; lay (to put or place): lay, laying, laid, have laid; sit (to rest in a sitting position): sit, sitting, sat, have sat; set (to put or place): set, setting, set, have set; rise (to go upward): rise, rising, rose, have risen; raise (to move something upward): raise, raising, raised, have raised.

Answer Key

Exercise 15 has been rewritten correctly below. Corrected verbs are marked with an asterisk (*). The misspelled words are underlined and respelled correctly. The misspelled words are *satisfied, plain, sweetly, pain,* and *always.*

A woman had *come to Carmel's Clothing Shop, where she *gave the clerk a very difficult time. The hours went by, and still she had not yet *begun to be <u>satisfied</u>. One by one, she inspected each article of clothing. She *asked the clerk questions regarding the article's size, color, workmanship, and durability. She wondered whether any items had ever *shrunk, and so on. Then she *laid each item down.

The clothes she had *set aside soon made a huge pile in the middle of the room. The clerk had *run into the back room many times searching for a particular item and had brought out more clothes to be *laid out for inspection. After hours of this, it was <u>plain</u> that the woman would never *choose anything. She had taken her time because she was shopping only for fun.

Finally, the woman *rose from the chair where she had *sat down to catch her breath.

She turned to leave. The clerk had not spoken for several minutes for fear of *bursting out and *raising the roof. After she had *blown a kiss to the clerk, the woman said <u>sweetly</u>, "I know you must think I'm a real <u>pain</u> to have *stolen your entire afternoon." The clerk smiled and replied, "The customer is <u>always</u> right, ma'am."

Leaving at last, the woman spied another dress she had not *known about. "Do you mind if I try on that dress in the window?" she *asked.

"Not at all, ma'am," replied the clerk. "But wouldn't you rather use the dressing room?"

Additional Activities

1. Have students define a regular verb and an irregular verb and give 10 examples of each.

2. Have students take turns writing a sentence on the board using a form of one of these words: *lie/lay, rise/raise, sit/set.* They may leave a blank and choose another student to fill in the correct form of the verb.

3. Read aloud sentences containing problem verbs. Make errors in some of the sentences. Ask the class whether each sentence is correct or incorrect.

4. Have students write original sentences using each problem verb *(lie/lay, rise/raise, sit/set)* in each verb tense.

5. Have students write a short story using as many of these words as possible:

rise	rose	has risen
raise	raised	has raised
lie	lay	has lain
lay	laid	has laid
sit	sat	has sat
set	set	has set

Have students exchange stories and check each other's work.

15. Principal Problems with Principal Parts

Directions: Look at each underlined verb in the story. If the verb is incorrect, cross out the incorrect form and write the correct form in the space above it. Circle the five misspelled words. Rewrite each word correctly in the Spelling Box.

A woman had <u>came</u> to Carmel's Clothing Shop, where she <u>give</u> the clerk a very difficult time. The hours <u>went</u> by, and still she had not yet <u>began</u> to be satisfyed. One by one, she <u>inspected</u> each article of clothing. She <u>ask</u> the clerk questions regarding the article's size, color, workmanship, and durability. She <u>wondered</u> whether any items had ever <u>shrank</u>, and so on. Then she <u>lay</u> each item down.

The clothes she had <u>sat</u> aside soon made a huge pile in the middle of the room. The clerk had <u>ran</u> into the back room many times searching for a particular item and had <u>brought</u> out more clothes to be <u>lain</u> out for inspection. After hours of this, it was plane that the woman would never <u>chose</u> anything. She had <u>taken</u> her time because she <u>was</u> shopping only for fun.

Finally, the woman <u>raised</u> from the chair where she had <u>set</u> down to catch her breath. She <u>turned</u> to leave. The clerk had not <u>spoken</u> for several minutes for fear of <u>busting</u> out and <u>rising</u> the roof. After she had <u>blowed</u> a kiss to the clerk, the woman said sweatly, "I know you must think I'm a real pane to have <u>stold</u> your entire afternoon."

The clerk <u>smiled</u> and <u>replied</u>, "The customer is all ways right, ma'am."

Leaving at last, the woman <u>spied</u> another dress she had not <u>knowed</u> about. "Do you mind if I try on that dress in the window?" she <u>ask</u>.

"Not at all, ma'am," <u>replied</u> the clerk. "But wouldn't you rather use the dressing room?"

SPELLING BOX	1. _____	2. _____
3. _____	4. _____	5. _____

35   *Find the Errors!*

16. Puzzling Pronouns

Background Information

This exercise includes practice on using the correct pronoun in a variety of situations. The rules follow:

Rule 1: Use nominative pronouns (*I, he, she, we,* and *they*) only as subjects or predicate nominatives.

(*Example:* I sang. John and I sang.)

Rule 2: Objective pronouns (*me, him, her, us,* and *them*) should be used only as objects. If the direct object is made up of a noun and a pronoun, an objective pronoun must still be used.

(*Example:* Sally helped me. Sally helped Bill and me.) **Note:** *You* is the same in both nominative and objective form.

Rule 3: When speaking of yourself and others, mention yourself last.

(*Example:* Joe and me, not me and Joe)

Rule 4: Don't use an apostrophe in possessive personal pronouns like *my, mine, her, his, hers, its, ours, our, your, yours, their, theirs.*

Rule 5: Verbs must agree with their pronoun subjects.

(*Example:* He doesn't live here. Not: He don't live here.)

Answer Key

Each pronoun error in the story has been corrected and marked with an asterisk (*). The misspelled words have been underlined and respelled correctly. The misspelled words are *clothes, guess, finally, paid,* and *apiece.*

A father and his 16-year-old twin sons, Bill and Will, were discussing *their family budget problems. Bill said, "It doesn't seem like much to you, Dad, but it's important to Will and me to have the right <u>clothes</u>."

"Yes," Will added, "*Bill and *I need money for our activities and hobbies, too."

"And," continued Bill, "may Will and I please borrow $25 for our dates Friday night?"

"Boys!" said their father sternly, "your mother and *I want you to have the best. You are *ours and it's great! But *there's no money tree in our backyard!"

The next evening the father was met at the door by his wife. She burst out excitedly, "<u>Guess</u> what, dear? You and *I have <u>finally</u> taught those sons of *ours the value of a dollar. All those lectures of *yours have <u>paid</u> off. Bill said that the thing Will and *he want for that upcoming birthday of *theirs will only cost $1 <u>apiece</u>."

"Well, well!" replied the father, "now that's what you and *I like to hear. And what do those boys of ours want?"

"Their own keys to the car!" answered the proud mother.

Additional Activities

1. Write sentences on the board in which students must choose between the following: *its* or *it's, their* or *they're, your* or *you're.*

2. Have students write five sentences with compound subjects and five sentences with compound direct objects. Each subject and object should contain at least one pronoun.

3. Write a list of compound subjects on the board, each containing at least one pronoun (e.g., *Bill and me, she and I . . .*). Have students use these in sentences correctly.

4. Challenge students to find examples of *its* and *it's* used incorrectly in newspapers or magazines. These words are often used incorrectly in advertisements as well. Have students bring these examples to class.

16. Puzzling Pronouns

Directions: There are several pronoun errors in the story below. Cross out each incorrect pronoun and write the correct pronoun above it. Circle the five misspelled words. Rewrite each word correctly in the Spelling Box.

A father and his 16-year-old twin sons, Bill and Will, were discussing they're family budget problems. Bill said, "It doesn't seem like much to you, Dad, but it's important to Will and me to have the right cloths."

"Yes," Will added, "Me and Bill need money for our activities and hobbies, too."

"And," continued Bill, "may Will and I please borrow $25 for our dates Friday night?"

"Boys!" said their father sternly, "your mother and me want you to have the best. You are our's and it's great! But theirs no money tree in our backyard!"

The next evening the father was met at the door by his wife. She burst out excitedly, "Gess what, dear? You and me have finaly taught those sons of our's the value of a dollar. All those lectures of your's have payed off. Bill said that the thing Will and him want for that upcoming birthday of there's will only cost $1 apeace."

"Well, well!" replied the father, "now that's what you and me like to hear. And what do those boys of ours want?"

"Their own keys to the car!" answered the proud mother.

SPELLING BOX	1. _____	2. _____
3. _____	4. _____	5. _____

37   *Find the Errors!*

17. Dangling Modifiers

Background Information

A dangling modifier is a modifying phrase or clause that does not clearly or sensibly modify any word in the sentence. When a modifying phrase begins a sentence, it should be followed by a comma, and then the word that the phrase modifies.

(*Example:* Playing soccer, I hurt my knee. Not: Playing soccer my knee was hurt.)

Answer Key

Answers may vary somewhat, but the following are sample corrections of these sentences. The misspelled words are *neighbor's, sale, announcement, vacuuming,* and *favorite.*

1. Mr. Schimmel saw his <u>neighbor's</u> garage <u>sale</u> sign nailed to a post.
2. I saw several sets of miniature animals arranged in the showcase.
3. correct (except "<u>announcement</u>" is misspelled)
4. A bee stung me while I was weeding the garden this morning. OR: While I was weeding the garden this morning, a bee stung me.
5. The baby woke up while I was vacuuming the hall. OR: Because I was <u>vacuuming</u> the hall, the baby woke up.
6. Climbing to the top of the Empire State Building, I saw the entire city of New York. OR: I saw the entire city of New York when I climbed to the top of the Empire State Building.
7. After we had hiked several hours in darkness, the moon rose and lit our way. OR: The moon rose and lit our way after we had hiked several hours in darkness.
8. correct (except "<u>favorite</u>" is misspelled)
9. His big toe was sprained when he was playing football. OR: Playing football, he sprained his big toe.
10. I was afraid the baby might fall since she was standing up in the high chair. OR: As the baby was standing up in the high chair, I was afraid he might fall.

Additional Activities

1. Write a list of introductory modifiers (e.g., *Whining loudly, Planning the party, Avoiding the mud puddle . . .*) on the board. Have students use these to write complete sentences, being sure to follow each introductory modifier by a word that it can sensibly modify.

2. Have students construct sentences with dangling modifiers. Read some of these aloud to the class. Allow students to correct the sentences.

17. Dangling Modifiers

Directions: Eight of the ten sentences below contain dangling modifiers. Correct these eight sentences by rewriting them in the space under the sentence. You may rearrange the words in the sentence or add words if needed to make the meaning of the sentence clear. Do not rewrite the sentences that are already correct. Circle the five misspelled words. Rewrite each word correctly in the Spelling Box.

1. Nailed to a post, Mr. Schimmel saw his nieghbor's garage sail sign.

2. Arranged in the showcase, I saw several sets of miniature animals.

3. Hurrying for my first class, I saw the anouncement on the wall.

4. Weeding the garden this morning, a bee stung me.

5. Vacuming the hall, the baby woke up.

6. Climbing to the top of the Empire State Building, the entire city of New York was visible.

7. After hiking several hours in darkness, the moon rose and lit our way.

8. Turning on the radio, I heard my favrite song.

9. Playing football, his big toe was sprained.

10. Standing up in the high chair, I was afraid the baby might fall.

SPELLING BOX		
	1. _____	2. _____
3. _____	4. _____	5. _____

18. Mystifying Modifiers

Background Information

Modifying phrases and clauses should be placed as near as possible to the words they modify. Otherwise, the meaning of the sentence can be distorted.

Example:

Incorrect: Inside the microwave oven I saw that the oatmeal was boiling over. (It sure would be uncomfortable sitting inside the microwave oven!)

Correct: I saw that the oatmeal was boiling over inside the microwave oven.

Answer Key

There may be more than one correct way to rewrite each sentence. Accept any reasonable answers. The following are sample corrections. The misspelled words are: *steak*, *retriever*, *transparent*, *flower*, and *binoculars*.

1. Mr. Alvarez ordered a medium rare <u>steak</u> and a green salad.
2. Terrell hoped her golden <u>retriever</u>, which she had carefully trained for months, would win first place in the dog show.
3. Ebony and I watched the spider, hanging from a nearly <u>transparent</u> web, approach her victim.
4. The theater next to the lake is showing that new action film.
5. correct
6. While I was still a preschooler, my aunt taught me the name of each <u>flower</u> in her garden.
7. The fire was extinguished by the volunteer fire department before any major damage could be done.
8. As I looked at the birds with my uncle's <u>binoculars</u>, I saw a golden eagle soar through the sky.
9. The teacher gave Keisha Saturday detention for breaking the rules.
10. correct
11. In our English class, Mario Lopez showed slides and told us about his spring vacation ski trip.
12. For a birthday present, a 10-speed bicycle was given to 10-year-old Arthur.

Additional Activities

1. Write a list of modifying phrases (e.g., *building a nest, under the counter, as a teenager*) on the board. Have students use these to write complete sentences, being sure to place the phrase as close as possible to the words it modifies.

2. Have students write comical examples of misplaced or dangling modifiers. Students may work as teams. Let the class vote on the most humorous examples and then correct all of them.

18. Mystifying Modifiers

Directions: Ten of the twelve sentences that follow contain misplaced or dangling modifiers. Two sentences are correct as written. Rewrite the ten incorrect sentences so they make sense. Put the modifying clause or phrase as close as possible to the words it modifies. Circle the five misspelled words. Rewrite each word correctly as you rewrite the sentence. Then write each corrected word in the Spelling Box.

1. Mr. Alvarez ordered a stake and a green salad medium rare.

2. Carefully trained for months, Terrell hoped her golden retreiver would win first place in the dog show.

3. Hanging from a nearly transparant web, Ebony and I watched the spider approach her victim.

4. The theater is showing that new action film next to the lake.

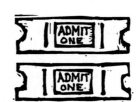

5. The small boy treasured his New York Yankees baseball cap, which was signed by members of the team.

6. While still a preschooler, my aunt taught me the name of each flour in her garden.

(continued)

18. **Mystifying Modifiers** *(continued)*

7. The fire was extinguished before any major damage could be done by the volunteer fire department.

8. Looking at the birds with my uncle's binoculers, a golden eagle soared through the sky.

9. Keisha was given Saturday detention when the rules were broken by the teacher.

10. Noticing the smell of something burning, I found that a pot was boiling over on the stove.

11. Mario Lopez showed slides and told us about his spring vacation ski trip in our English class.

12. For a birthday present, a bicycle was given to 10-year-old Arthur with 10 speeds.

SPELLING BOX	1. _____	2. _____
3. _____	4. _____	5. _____

 Find the Errors!

19. Practice Those Principles!
20. More Principle Practice
21. Proofreading Practice

Background Information

These are review exercises. Exercise 19 is a review of Exercises 14–18. Exercises 20 and 21 are a review of Exercises 1–18.

Answer Key for Exercise 19

The misspelled words are *professor, methods, suggested, agreement,* and *whole.*

1.	a	<u>use</u>
2.	c	<u>Using</u> his <u>university</u> <u>teaching</u> <u>methods</u>
3.	a	<u>approach</u>
4.	b	<u>I</u> and <u>the</u> <u>others</u>
5.	c	<u>Agreeing</u> <u>to</u> <u>this</u> <u>plan</u>
6.	a	<u>begun</u>
7.	a	<u>jump</u>
8.	a	<u>don't</u>
9.	c	<u>winding</u> <u>up</u>
10.	b	<u>you</u> <u>and</u> <u>me</u>
11.	b	<u>him</u>

Answer Key for Exercise 20

Exercise 20 is rewritten correctly below. Answers may vary somewhat. The following are sample corrections. The misspelled words are: *through, neither, responsible, neighbors,* and *breath.*

Driving <u>west</u> on the <u>Long Island Expressway</u>, the 10-<u>year</u>-old boy listened to his <u>father</u> talk about the good old days.

"You know, Jamal," said his dad, "when <u>Abraham Lincoln</u> was a boy, he had to walk 10 miles to Big Spring School <u>through</u> deep snowdrifts. <u>Neither</u> rain nor cold <u>was</u> able to slow him down."

Looking at the passing scenery, <u>Dad</u> was silent for a minute. Then <u>Dad</u> took up where <u>he'd</u> left off.

"Young <u>Lincoln</u> worked hard around the house, too. At seven <u>Abe</u> <u>was</u> <u>given</u> an ax.

He, like other boys his age, <u>was</u> <u>responsible</u> for keeping the wood box full." Warming to his subject, Dad continued, "<u>Abe</u> planted crops, and he picked wild berries. It was <u>Abe's</u> job to walk the mile to the spring and carry water home when the well ran dry. At night, hungry for knowledge, <u>Abe</u> <u>studied</u> <u>his</u> <u>books</u> for hours. Sometimes Abe worked for <u>neighbors</u> for <u>twenty-five</u> cents a day. And by law Abe had to give the money he earned to his <u>father</u>." Pausing for a <u>breath</u>, <u>Dad</u> <u>slowed</u> the <u>car</u> to a stop. "Well, <u>Son</u>, what do you think of that?"

"<u>It's</u> a good story, <u>Dad</u>," the boy replied, laughing. "Just remember that when Abraham Lincoln was your age, he was president!"

Answer Key for Exercise 21

Exercise 20 is rewritten correctly below. Answers may vary somewhat. The following are sample corrections. The misspelled words are *prettiest, popular, gorgeous, introduce,* and *weak.*

Joey Allegrezza had a crush on the <u>prettiest</u>, most <u>popular</u> girl in the freshman class. She, more than any of the other girls, <u>was</u> a real knockout. She had beautiful hair, <u>gorgeous</u> eyes, and a winning smile.

<u>She</u> <u>and</u> <u>Joey</u> <u>were</u> in the same <u>American</u> history, <u>Spanish</u>, and economics classes. However, he had never gotten up the nerve to <u>introduce</u> himself.

Standing behind her in the cafeteria lunch line one day, <u>he</u> <u>felt</u> his knees grow <u>weak</u> and his heart grow faint. He, like most of the other boys in the class, <u>was</u> unsure what to say to this beautiful girl.

Just then, the girl turned and spoke to him. Pointing to one food item in the serving line, she asked, "What do you suppose they call *that*?"

"Uh, that's Joey Allegrezza. And, by the way, I'm carrot salad."

19. Practice Those Principles!

Directions: Each sentence below contains one major error. Write the letter of the error next to the sentence. (You will use each letter more than once.) If the error is an incorrect verb or a pronoun error, underline the error. If the error is a dangling or misplaced modifier, underline the misplaced phrase. Circle the five misspelled words. Rewrite each word correctly in the Spelling Box.

a. incorrect verb

b. pronoun error

c. dangling or misplaced modifier

_____ 1. The new high school algebra teacher use to be a university math professer.

_____ 2. Using his university teaching methuds, the students were totally lost.

_____ 3. One day, a group of students approach the teacher after class and explained that he was going too fast, and no one could take notes.

_____ 4. One student sugested, "I and the others would like you to slow down and write the equations on the board for us to copy."

_____ 5. Agreeing to this plan, the teacher's eyes were kind.

_____ 6. But the next day he begun to lecture on a facet of algebra which he found especially fascinating.

_____ 7. His explanation went faster and faster as he jump about from one equation to another.

_____ 8. He don't remember his agrement with the students.

_____ 9. Winding up, the class was dazed.

_____ 10. The professor exclaimed, "And so, you and me can see that the hole process is as obvious as the fact that 2 + 2 = 4!"

_____ 11. Suddenly remembering what his students and him had agreed, he turned swiftly to the chalkboard and wrote carefully, "2 + 2 = 4."

SPELLING BOX	1. _____	2. _____
3. _____	4. _____	5. _____

20. More Principle Practice

Directions: Rewrite the following story on a separate sheet of paper. Correct all punctuation and capitalization errors. Correct any verb-usage errors, incorrect pronouns, and dangling and misplaced modifiers. Circle the five spelling errors, and rewrite each word correctly in the Spelling Box.

Driving West on the long island expressway, the 10 year old boy listened to his Father talk about the good old days.

"You know Jamal" said his Dad "When abraham lincoln was a boy he had to walk 10 miles to Big Spring school threw deep snowdrifts. Niether rain nor cold were able to slow him down."

Looking at the passing scenery, the car was silent for a minute. Then dad took up where hed left off.

"Young lincoln worked hard around the house, too. At seven his Dad gave him an ax. He, like other boys his age, were responsable for keeping the wood box full." Warming to his subject, Dad continued, "abe planted crops and he picked wild berries. It was Abes job to walk the mile to the spring and carry water home when the well ran dry. At night, hungry for knowledge, his books were studied for hours. Sometimes Abe worked for nieghbors for twenty five cents a day. And by law Abe had to give the money he earned to his Father." Pausing for a breathe, the car slowed to a stop. "Well, son, what do you think of that?"

"Its a good story dad," the boy replied, laughing. "Just remember that when Abraham Lincoln was your age, he was president!"

SPELLING BOX	1. _____	2. _____
3. _____	4. _____	5. _____

45   *Find the Errors!*

21. Proofreading Practice

Directions: Rewrite the story below, correcting all errors. There are five spelling errors; correct them as you rewrite the story. Then place each corrected word in the Spelling Box.

Joey Allegrezza had a crush on the prettyest most populer girl in the freshman class. She, more than any of the other girls, were a real knockout. She had beautiful hair gorgous eyes and a winning smile.

Joey and her was in the same american history spanish and economics classes. However he had never gotten up the nerve to introduse himself.

Standing behind her in the cafeteria lunch line one day his knees felt  week and his heart felt faint. He like most of the other boys in the class were unsure what to say to this beautiful girl.

Just then the girl turned and spoke to him. Pointing to one food item in the serving line she asked What do you suppose they call *that*

Uh thats Joey Allegrezza. And by the way Im carrot salad.

SPELLING BOX	1. _____	2. _____
3. _____	4. _____	5. _____

46 *Find the Errors!*

22. The Incomplete Thought

Background Information

This exercise deals with the correction of sentence fragments according to the following rules:

Rule 1: A sentence fragment may lack a subject, a verb, or both a subject and a verb.

Examples:

Hopped along quietly. (no subject)
The three college students and their mothers. (no verb)
Across the field. (no subject or verb)

Rule 2: A fragment may sometimes be corrected by using correct punctuation.

Example:

Incorrect: I enjoy playing tennis. Especially in the fall.

Correct: I enjoy playing tennis, especially in the fall.

Rule 3: Fragments may sometimes incorrectly contain the infinitive or participle form of a verb.

Examples:

Incorrect: George skating all afternoon

Incorrect: Mark to be the chairman.

Rule 4: In conversation, fragments are often used for natural sounding speech.

Answer Key

There is more than one correct way to rewrite the letter. The following is one way the letter could be rewritten correctly. The misspelled words have been underlined and rewritten correctly. They are *hear, instead, hoping, whiling,* and *hours.*

My dearest love,

For one touch of your delicate hand, I could swim the mighty ocean. I would climb the highest mountain just to see your beautiful, glowing face from afar. I would lie on a bed of nails or walk over hot coals to <u>hear</u> one word from your lovely lips. Whenever I think of you, my love, my heart pounds wildly, and my knees grow weak.

I wish I could be with you now <u>instead</u> of so far away. I can only hope you feel the same way. I hope you are waiting and <u>hoping</u> to hear from me. Meanwhile, I am sitting by the telephone, <u>whiling</u> away the <u>hours</u>.

Yours always, Freddy

P.S. I'll be over Saturday night to see you if it doesn't rain.

Additional Activities

1. Write some sentence fragments on the board. Students are to use these to make complete sentences.

2. Write sentences and fragments on the board or read them aloud. Have students indicate whether each is a sentence or a fragment.

3. On the board write the fragment *"Almost every day at* _____ (your school's name) . . ."* Have students complete the sentence. Point out how many different ways it can be completed.

4. Have students write and illustrate a sentence fragment in a humorous way. For example, for the fragment "Bill caught," the drawing could show Bill going to great lengths to catch nothing.

22. The Incomplete Thought

Directions: The letter below contains some sentence fragments and some complete sentences. Rewrite the story in the space below using only complete sentences. You will need to add words to change some fragments into sentences. You may combine fragments or a sentence and a fragment to make a complete sentence. Circle the five misspelled words. Rewrite each word correctly in the Spelling Box.

My dearest love,

For one touch of your delicate hand. I could swim the mighty ocean. Your beautiful glowing face. I would climb the highest mountain just to see from afar. Lying on a bed of nails. I would walk over hot coals to here one word from your lovely lips. Whenever I think of you, my love. My heart pounds wildly and my knees grow weak.

To be with you now insted of so far away. I can only hope you feel the same way. You waiting and hopping to hear from me. Sitting by the telephone, whileing away the ours.

Yours always, Freddy

SPELLING BOX	1. _____	2. _____
3. _____	4. _____	5. _____

                   Find the Errors!

23. A Word Traffic Jam

Background Information

In this exercise, students correct run-on sentences. A run-on sentence is defined as two or more sentences separated only by a comma or by no mark of punctuation. Here are some ways to correct run-on sentences.

Rule 1: Break run-ons into separate sentences by using correct punctuation and capitalization.

Rule 2: When possible, combine parts of the run-on sentence by using compound subjects, verbs, predicate nominatives, or direct objects.

Examples:

Compound direct object:

Incorrect: The children played jacks they played hopscotch too.

Correct: The children played jacks and hopscotch.

Compound verb:

Incorrect: The boy hit the ball he ran after it.

Correct: The boy hit the ball and ran after it.

Compound subject:

Incorrect: Billy will go to the fair so will Johnny.

Correct: Billy and Johnny will go to the fair.

Compound predicate nominative:

Incorrect: Mr. Jones is the owner of this store he is also the manager.

Correct: Mr. Jones is the owner and manager of this store.

Rule 3: Appositives may be used to combine sentence parts.

Example:

Incorrect: Dr. Jones is my dentist he is also my neighbor.

Correct: Dr. Jones, my dentist, is my neighbor.

Answer Key

In some instances, there may be more than one way to correct the run-on sentences. Accept any reasonable answer. The misspelled words are *course, already, unfortunately, entrance,* and *it's.*

Jamila was taking a 7:30 A.M. <u>course</u> at Salt Lake City Junior College<u>. It</u> was all the way across town from where she lived. She lived near the mountains<u>, sharing</u> an apartment with three other girls<u>. None</u> of the others had such an early class!

<u>Already</u> Jamila had missed the class several times<u>,</u> and the professor was very annoyed<u>. He</u> even threatened to fail her if she missed class again.

Waking up a bit late one morning, Jamila rushed across town<u>. She</u> arrived at class just in time<u>. Unfortunately</u> she parked in a no-parking zone near the <u>entrance. When</u> the class was over, she found that her car had been towed.

Jamila called the police<u>. They</u> asked her to describe the car, which she did. <u>"It's</u> a dark-green 1982 Plymouth Fury <u>with</u> a lot of rust on the hood and trunk<u>. It</u> has a big crack on the front windshield<u>,</u> and the hubcaps are missing. It has a basket of dirty laundry on the back seat. (correct) On the rear bumper is a bumper sticker <u>reading</u> 'Don't laugh. <u>It's</u> paid for.'"

"Well, young lady," the dispatcher said kindly, "don't worry. I'm sure the car hasn't been stolen!" (correct)

Additional Activities

1. Make up run-on sentences for the students to correct.
2. Read some sentences, fragments, and run-on sentences aloud. Have students tell how many sentences they hear in what you read.
3. Have each student write a paragraph with no punctuation. Students then exchange papers and punctuate the stories correctly.

23. A Word Traffic Jam

Directions: The story below contains some run-on sentences and some sentences that are correct. Rewrite the story, correcting any run-on sentences. Do not rewrite any sentences that are already correct. Circle the five misspelled words, and spell each word correctly as you rewrite the story. Then write each corrected word in the Spelling Box.

Jamila was taking a 7:30 A.M. coarse at Salt Lake City Junior College, it was all the way across town from where she lived. She lived near the mountains and she shared an apartment with three other girls and none of the others had such an early class!

All ready Jamila had missed the class several times and the professor was very annoyed, he even threatened to fail her if she missed class again.

Waking up a bit late one morning, Jamila rushed across town and she arrived at class just in time but unfortunatly she parked in a no-parking zone near the enterance and when the class was over she found that her car had been towed.

Jamila called the police, they asked her to describe the car, which she did, "It's a dark-green 1982 Plymouth Fury and it has a lot of rust on the hood and trunk and it has a big crack on the front windshield and the hubcaps are missing. It has a basket of dirty laundry on the back seat. On the rear bumper is a bumper sticker, it reads, 'Don't laugh its paid for.'"

"Well, young lady," the dispatcher said kindly, "don't worry. I'm sure the car hasn't been stolen!"

SPELLING BOX	1. _____	2. _____
3. _____	4. _____	5. _____

24. Proofreading for Sentence Sense

Background Information

This exercise is a review of Exercises 22 and 23.

Answer Key

The misspelled words are *editor, absolutely, ladies, raised,* and *charities.*

Nina Washington had just graduated from college. She had majored in journalism, so she was happy when she landed her first job as a reporter for the society section of the paper. This was an area she found fascinating.

When Nina began work, she was cautioned by her <u>editor</u> to check and double-check the accuracy of each story. The editor told her to be certain anything she wrote was <u>absolutely</u> true. The paper could be sued otherwise. The editor suggested the reporter use words such as *claimed, alleged, rumored, reported,* and so on, in her stories. This is the story Nina wrote on the town's social event of the year, the gala charity ball:

"A gala charity ball was given on Friday. The ball was attended by all the town's allegedly respectable <u>ladies</u> and their reputedly fashionable husbands. It was rumored that Dr. and Mrs. Jones hosted the alleged party, which they claimed was a big success. The charity ball <u>raised</u> $10,000, all of which was supposedly given to local <u>charities.</u>"

24. Proofreading for Sentence Sense

Directions: The story below contains sentence fragments, run-on sentences, and correct sentences. Rewrite the story, correcting any sentence fragments or run-on sentences. Add words to sentence fragments if needed. Circle the five misspelled words and spell each word correctly as you rewrite the story. Then write each corrected word in the Spelling Box.

Nina Washington had just graduated from college and she had majored in journalism so she was happy when she landed her first job; it was as a reporter for the society section of the paper. An area she found fascinating.

When Nina began work, she was cautioned by her editer. To check and double-check the accuracy of each story. The editor told her to be certain anything she wrote was absolutely true the paper could be sued otherwise. The editor suggested the reporter use words such as *claimed, alleged, rumored, reported,* and so on, in her stories. This story on the town's social event of the year, the gala charity ball:

"A gala charity ball was given on Friday, the ball was attended by all the town's allegedly respectable ladys and their reputedly fashionable husbands. It was rumored that Dr. and Mrs. Jones hosted the alleged party they claimed was a big success. The charity ball razed $10,000. All of which supposedly given to local charitys."

SPELLING BOX	1. _____	2. _____
3. _____	4. _____	5. _____

   Find the Errors!

25. The Spice of Life

Background Information

This exercise gives students practice in varying sentence constructions. The original version of the story consists mainly of short, choppy sentences. Students need to rewrite the story, using a variety of sentence constructions. Here are some rules for doing this:

Rule 1: Vary the kinds of sentences you write, using simple, compound, and complex sentences.

Examples:

Simple: We visited Paris this summer.
Compound: We saw the Eiffel Tower, and we visited the Louvre.
Complex: After we had dinner in an elegant restaurant, we climbed Montmartre to Sacre Coeur.

Rule 2: Vary sentence length as you write. Avoid too many short sentences. Also avoid long, stringy sentences.

Rule 3: Use different sentence beginnings. Avoid putting the subject first in every sentence. Sometimes start with a modifying word, phrase, or clause.

Examples of various sentence beginnings:

Frightened, the puppy ran away. (Beginning with an adjective)
Unfortunately, the game was rained out. (Adverb)
On the other side of the street stands the theater. (Prepositional phrase)
To be helpful, I washed the dishes. (Infinitive phrase)
While I waited, the jeweler fixed my watch. (Subordinate clause)

Answer Key

There are many ways this story could be rewritten to provide variety in length and form of the sentences. One corrected example is provided. The words misspelled in the story have been underlined and rewritten correctly. The misspelled words are *quiet, wagged, silence, already,* and *beaten.*

A student entering the high school cafeteria saw a large, <u>quiet</u> crowd watching a girl. She was playing checkers with a large dog seated across from her.

The dog played well. Holding a checker in his mouth, he jumped some of the girl's checkers. He barked and <u>wagged</u> his tail excitedly.

The girl jumped one of the dog's checkers. He whined a bit, but otherwise he appeared to be a good sport. The game went on.

The students watched in awestruck <u>silence</u>. One student gasped, "Hey, that's sure a smart dog you have there!"

"Not so smart!" answered the girl. "I've <u>already</u> <u>beaten</u> him four times out of five."

Additional Activities

1. Write a story on the board in which every sentence begins with the subject. Have students rewrite the story with the subjects in different places, following the examples on the teacher guide page.

2. Write a list of modifiers on the board (e.g., alone, tired and frightened, suddenly . . .). Have students use these to begin original sentences.

3. Write a paragraph on the board which consists wholly of short, simple sentences. Have students rewrite it, using some complex and compound sentences.

4. Have students write paragraphs on topics of their own choosing, being careful to vary sentence types.

5. Write examples of long, stringy sentences on the board. Have students rewrite these using better style.

25. The Spice Of Life

Directions: The story below has been separated into five sections. Each section consists of short, choppy sentences with no variety in length or form. Rewrite each section using a variety of sentence patterns. You may wish to combine some sentences to form compound or complex sentences. Circle the five misspelled words, and spell the words correctly as you rewrite the story.

A student entered the high school cafeteria. He saw a large crowd. The crowd was quite. The crowd was watching a girl. The girl was playing checkers. She was playing checkers with a large dog. The dog was seated across from her.

The dog played well. The dog held a checker in his mouth. The dog jumped some of the girl's checkers. The dog barked. The dog waged his tail. He wagged his tail excitedly.

The girl jumped one of the dog's checkers. The dog whined a bit. Otherwise, the dog appeared to be a good sport. The game went on.

The students watched. They watched in awestruck silense. One student gasped. He gasped, "Hey, that's sure a smart dog you have there!"

"Not so smart!" answered the girl. "I've all ready beeten him. I've beaten him four times out of five."

54   *Find the Errors!*

26. What's the Correct Time?

Background Information

This exercise deals with eliminating unnecessary shifts in verb tense.

Rule 1: Avoid needless changes from one tense to another.

Example:

Incorrect: Billy hit the ball and rushes to retrieve it.

Correct: Billy hit the ball and rushed to retrieve it.

Rule 2: Use the perfect tenses to express action that has been completed or to show the sequence of events.

Example:

Incorrect: I felt sorry that he broke his toy.

Correct: I felt sorry that he had broken his toy.

Answer Key

Exercise 26 has been rewritten below. The first paragraph should be in the present tense, since it describes a place existing in the present. For the rest of the story, students should choose one or the other tense and use it consistently. In the last paragraph of the story, the three verbs must be in the past tense, because of the meaning of the sentences. The misspelled words have been underlined and rewritten correctly. The misspelled words are *complete, partially, guide, million,* and *site.*

Dinosaur National Monument <u>is</u> located in Jensen, Utah. Thousands of dinosaur bones are (no change) at this amazing site. The Visitor Center <u>displays</u> dinosaur bones in their natural setting as they were (no change) actually found in the rocks. This exhibit <u>is</u> spectacular and attracts (no change) many tourists each year.

A group of tourists was visiting (no change) Dinosaur National Monument. Everywhere they <u>looked</u> <u>were</u> piles and piles of dinosaur bones. The tourists <u>were</u> especially interested in the <u>complete</u> dinosaur skeleton which was (no change) still <u>partially</u> buried in the rocky hillside.

One of the tourists talked (no change) to an old man who <u>acted</u> as a volunteer <u>guide</u> for the museum. He <u>asked</u> the man how old the dinosaur bones <u>were</u>. The man <u>answered</u> that they were (no change) one <u>million</u> five and one-half years old.

The tourist was surprised (no change) that the bones could (no change) be dated so precisely. But the man <u>explained</u> the reason. An archeologist had visited (no change) the <u>site</u> and determined (no change) the bones were (no change) one million years old. That visit took (no change) place exactly five and one-half years ago!

Additional Activities

1. Write a paragraph on the board containing shifts in tense. Have students rewrite it correctly.

2. Have students construct sentences with shifts in tense. They may then take turns writing these on the board and correcting them.

   Example: Tam turned the key and starts the car.

26. What's the Correct Time?

Directions: The story below contains many inconsistent verb tense "jumps." For each paragraph, choose the tense that makes the most sense. Then change any verbs to make them consistent with your choice. Circle the five misspelled words, and spell each word correctly as you rewrite the story. Then write each corrected word in the Spelling Box.

Dinosaur National Monument was located in Jensen, Utah. Thousands of dinosaur bones are at this amazing site. The Visitor Center displayed dinosaur bones in their natural setting as they were actually found in the rocks. This exhibit was spectacular and attracts many tourists each year.

A group of tourists was visiting Dinosaur National Monument. Everywhere they look are piles and piles of dinosaur bones. The tourists are especially interested in the compleat dinosaur skeleton which was still partialy buried in the rocky hillside.

One of the tourists talked to an old man who acts as a volunteer gide for the museum. He asks the man how old the dinosaur bones are. The man answers that they were one milion five and one-half years old.

The tourist was surprised that the bones could be dated so precisely. But the man explains the reason. An archeologist had visited the sight and determined the bones were one million years old. That visit took place exactly five and one-half years ago!

SPELLING BOX	1. _____	2. _____
3. _____	4. _____	5. _____

27. Give It Life!

Background Information

In this exercise, students practice rewriting sentences containing "tired" vocabulary, according to the following rules:

Rule 1: Use interesting synonyms for tired adjectives (e.g., *nice, wonderful, swell, great . . .*).

Example:

Uninteresting: A nice book

Better: A thrilling suspense tale

Rule 2: Use specific rather than general words to create a picture for the reader.

Example:

Uninteresting: The dog walked beside the man.

Better: The huge Saint Bernard lumbered along beside his elderly master.

Rule 3: Use strong rather than weak verbs.

Example:

Uninteresting: She said, "Help!"

Better: She screamed, "Help!"

Answer Key

Answers will vary. Below are some suggestions. The misspelled words are *library, it's, maybe, too,* and *interesting.*

1. A <u>teenager</u> lived in a <u>tiny</u> town. They closed the town <u>library</u> because someone took out the book.
2. An <u>exasperated</u> teacher <u>lectured</u> a <u>seventh-grade</u> student: "We start class when <u>it's</u> exactly 8:00 A.M."
   The <u>cooperative</u> student replied, "That's <u>agreeable</u> with me, but if I'm not here by then, go ahead and start without me."
3. The <u>pleasant</u> teacher <u>inquired</u>, "How do you spell *occasion?*"
   The student tried, "*O K A S H U N.*"
   <u>Discouraged</u>, the teacher pointed out, "The <u>dictionary</u> spells it *O C C A S I O N.*

"You didn't ask how the <u>dictionary</u> spells it," the student replied. "You asked how I spell it!
4. Marty asked, "Do you think a <u>popular</u> girl like Helen could be <u>content</u> with an <u>everyday</u> guy like me?"
   George retorted, "<u>Maybe</u>, if he wasn't <u>too</u> much like you."
5. A <u>spaceship</u> from <u>Venus</u> tried to land in <u>New York City</u> <u>last</u> <u>Tuesday</u> but couldn't find a parking space. So they had to move on to <u>Boston</u>.
6. <u>Four-year-old</u> Jon and <u>three-year-old</u> Hannah were watching <u>cartoons</u> on television. At the most <u>interesting</u> part, Jon turned off the set.
   "Why did you do that?" <u>yelled</u> Hannah.
   "I need to go to the bathroom," <u>explained</u> Jon, "and I don't want to miss anything!"

Additional Activities

1. Write sentences containing tired, overused, and general words on the board. As an oral activity, see how many interesting variations students can come up with, or have students rewrite the sentences using vivid vocabulary.

2. Have students write a descriptive paragraph in which they use adjectives and nouns that give a clear and exact picture.

3. Have students think of nouns to fit these categories: general, specific, and more specific (e.g., *clothing, shoe, sandal*). Discuss how the use of more specific nouns adds interest.

4. Write overused words (e.g., *go, say, look, nice, bad*) on the board. See how many interesting synonyms the class can list.

5. Have students write a paragraph about someone in action (e.g., a runner, a football player) using specific, vivid verbs.

6. Have students write a travel brochure about your town, state, or an attraction nearby. They are to use a variety of

adjectives to make the place sound exciting to visit.

7. Have students choose a picture from a magazine. They are to write a story or poem about the picture, making their vocabulary lively and interesting.

8. Have students bring an example of good descriptive writing, either prose or poetry, to class to read aloud.

9. Bring an interesting picture or object to class. The item should be abstract or open to interpretation. Have students write a paragraph describing it, using lively vocabulary.

27. Give It Life!

Directions: Replace each underlined "tired word" in the sentences below with a more descriptive or interesting word or phrase. Write the word you choose above the "tired word" it will replace. Circle the five misspelled words, and rewrite each word correctly in the Spelling Box.

1. A <u>young</u> <u>person</u> lived in a <u>small</u> town. They closed the town libary because someone took out the book.

2. An <u>unhappy</u> teacher <u>said</u> to a <u>young</u> student: "We start class when its exactly 8:00 A.M." The <u>nice</u> student replied, "That's <u>OK</u> with me, but if I'm not here by then, go ahead and start without me."

3. The <u>nice</u> teacher <u>said</u>, "How do you spell *occasion*?"
   The student tried, "*O K A S H U N.*"
   <u>Sad</u>, the teacher pointed out, "The <u>book</u> spells it *O C C A S I O N.*"
   "You didn't ask how the <u>book</u> spells it," the student replied. "You asked how I spell it!"

4. Marty asked, "Do you think a <u>nice</u> girl like Helen could be <u>happy</u> with a <u>nice</u> guy like me?"
   George retorted, "May be, if he wasn't to much like you."

5. A <u>vehicle</u> from <u>another</u> <u>planet</u> tried to land in <u>a</u> <u>big</u> <u>city</u> <u>one</u> <u>day</u> but couldn't find a parking space. So they had to move on to <u>another</u> <u>big</u> <u>city</u>.

6. <u>Little</u> Jon and <u>little</u> Hannah were watching <u>a</u> <u>show</u> on television.
   At the most <u>intresting</u> part, Jon turned off the set.
   "Why did you do that?" <u>said</u> Hannah.
   "I need to go to the bathroom," <u>said</u> Jon, "and I don't want to miss anything!"

SPELLING BOX	1. _____	2. _____
3. _____	4. _____	5. _____

28. Weeding Out Wordiness

Background Information

This exercise shows some ways students may reduce wordiness in their writing. These rules are used:

Rule 1: Avoid the use of double negatives.
Example:
Wrong: Joe does not never do no work.
Better: Joe does no work.

Rule 2: Eliminate superfluous words.
Example:
Wrong: In my opinion I think he's right.
Better: I think he's right.

Rule 3: Avoid unnecessary repetition of ideas.
Example:
Wrong: Last summer I went camping during the summer.
Better: Last summer I went camping.

Rule 4: Some clauses and phrases may be reduced to a single word.
Example:
Wordy: We met a girl who is a native of Mexico.
Better: We met a Mexican girl.

Rule 5: Avoid writing in an unnatural, over-written style. Too many big words, foreign words, flowery phrases, etc., make writing awkward and hard to understand.
Example:
Representative Maury Maverick of Texas coined the term *gobbledygook* after reading this sentence in the United States government manual: "Illumination is required to be extinguished upon vacating these premises."
(Better: "Turn out the light when you leave.")

Answer Key

Answers will vary. Suggested answers are given below. The misspelled words are *pollution, opinion, again, conclusion,* and *review.*

1. Omit the words <u>not</u> <u>never</u> <u>do</u>, or omit the words <u>never</u> <u>do</u> <u>no</u>. (Isabel does no work.

OR: Isabel does not work.
OR: Isabel never works.)

2. Omit the phrase <u>I</u> <u>think</u> or the phrase <u>in</u> <u>my</u> <u>opinion</u>. (Mr. Osawa is right about <u>pollution</u> control in my <u>opinion</u>. OR: I think Mr. Osawa is right about pollution control.)

3. Omit the words <u>as</u> <u>far</u> <u>below</u> <u>as</u> <u>we</u> <u>could</u> <u>see</u>. Omit the words <u>that</u> <u>wee</u> <u>tiny</u> <u>little</u> <u>group</u> <u>of</u> <u>buildings</u> <u>which</u> <u>make</u> <u>up</u>. (Far below in the distance we saw Whitten Junior High School.)

4. Omit the words <u>again</u> and <u>before</u>. (Please repeat what you said.)

5. Omit the words <u>again</u> to <u>another</u> <u>term</u> <u>of</u> <u>office</u>. (Congressperson Lightfoot was reelected.)

6. Omit the words <u>final</u> and either <u>in</u> <u>the</u> <u>long</u> <u>run</u> or <u>eventually</u>. (My <u>conclusion</u> is that eventually we'll win. OR: My conclusion is that in the long run we'll win.)

7. Omit the words <u>she</u>, <u>together</u>, and <u>their</u> <u>musi-cal</u> <u>talents</u> <u>and</u> <u>abilities</u> <u>whatever</u> <u>instrument</u> <u>they</u> <u>are</u> <u>good</u> <u>at</u>. (My sister has some friends who have combined to form a band. OR: My sister has some friends who have formed a band.)

8. Answers will vary. (Willie prefers to study for tests alone so he can <u>review</u> the material rather than joining a study group. OR: Willie prefers to study for exams by himself so he can review the material alone instead of joining a study group.)

9. Many young students try to impress their teachers by using an artificial style with long, scholarly words, foreign phrases, and lengthy sentences.

10. No smoking when you leave this area.

Additional Activities

1. Write examples of wordy sentences on the board. Have students rewrite the sentences in a more concise style.

2. Have students take turns writing wordy sentences on the board. Other students may then correct each sentence.

28. Weeding Out Wordiness

Directions: Each sentence below is wordy. Cross out the repetitious words or phrases in each sentence and make any other necessary changes. DO NOT change the meaning of the sentence. Circle the five misspelled words in sentences 1–8 (there are none in sentences 9 and 10) and rewrite each word correctly in the Spelling Box.

1. Isabel does not never do no work.

2. I think Mr. Osawa is right about polution control in my opinyun.

3. Far below in the distance as far below as we could see we saw that wee tiny little group of buildings which make up Whitten Junior High School.

4. Please repeat agin what you said before.

5. Congressperson Lightfoot was reelected again to another term of office.

6. My final conclushun is that eventually in the long run we'll win.

7. My sister she has some friends who have combined together their musical talents and abilities whatever instrument they are good at to form a band.

8. Willie he prefers to study for tests or exams alone by himself so he can reveiw the material again by himself, rather than as opposed to joining a study group.

Directions: Rewrite the following sentences, expressing the same idea in a simpler style.

9. Multitudinous young scholars seek to impress their educators by affecting an artificial, flowery, cumbersome style using lengthy, pedantic words, exotic phrases, and elongated sentences.

10. Smoking materials are required to be extinguished before you vacate the premises.

SPELLING BOX	1. _____	2. _____
3. _____	4. _____	5. _____

           Find the Errors!

29. Be Original!

Background Information

This exercise deals with eliminating clichés and trite expressions. Clichés are words or expressions that are so overused they have lost their meaning and effectiveness. These words and expressions are common in conversation but should be avoided in writing.

Examples of word clichés include: *nice, interesting,* and *wonderful.*

Examples of clichéd expressions include: *as busy as a bee, accidents will happen, as dull as dishwater.*

Answer Key

Answers will vary. Suggested replacements for the underlined clichés in the story are given below. The misspelled words are *philosophy, minute, reigned, attempt,* and *would.*

all work and no play makes Jack a dull boy	he wasn't having enough fun
two heads were better than one	maybe he could help
teach an old dog new tricks	give him some pointers
on the right track	sure to be successful
as easy as falling off a log	not so hard
barking up the wrong tree	go wrong
a mile a minute	nonstop
the cat's out of the bag	That's my secret!
like bumps on a log	silently
trying to keep his head above water	trying to start the conversation
taking the bull by the horns	persistently
get the ball rolling	get the conversation moving
feeling his ship going down	desperately
like a drowning man who clutches at every twig	wracking his brain for yet another conversation starter
jumping out of the frying pan into the fire	going from bad to worse

Additional Activities

1. Have each student list five words, five comparisons, and five expressions that are overused to the point of being clichés (e.g., *nice, as old as the hills, have a good day*). Have students read their lists aloud, or compile a list on the board.

2. Write sentences containing clichés on the board. Have students rewrite these, using more vivid language.
   Examples:
   He was a nice man.
   The children were as busy as bees.

3. Have students write product ad slogans in two versions. The first version should use a cliché. The second version should use interesting or specific vocabulary. Read these aloud in class. Discuss why the second version is better.
   Example:
   "Fair Hair Shampoo will make your hair as clean as a whistle." (cliché) OR: "Fair Hair Shampoo's scientifically proven cleaning ingredients will keep your hair healthy and lustrous."

29. Be Original!

Directions: The story below contains a number of clichés. Rewrite each underlined cliché in the space above it, using your own words. One is done for you. Circle the five misspelled words, and rewrite each word correctly in the Spelling Box.

he wasn't having enough fun.

Jack never had any dates. He decided <u>all work</u> <u>and</u> <u>no play</u> <u>makes</u> <u>Jack</u> <u>a</u> <u>dull</u> <u>boy</u>. His

friend had lots of dates, so Jack decided that <u>two</u> <u>heads</u> <u>were</u> <u>better</u> <u>than</u> <u>one</u>. Perhaps his friend

could <u>teach</u> <u>an</u> <u>old</u> <u>dog</u> <u>new</u> tricks.

  "You're <u>on</u> <u>the</u> <u>right</u> <u>track</u> now," said the friend. "Talking to girls is <u>as</u> <u>easy</u> <u>as</u> <u>falling</u> <u>off</u> <u>a</u>

<u>log</u>. You won't <u>be</u> <u>barking</u> <u>up</u> <u>the</u> <u>wrong</u> <u>tree</u> if you use one of these three topics to start a conver-

sation: relatives, food, or philosofy. Just make a comment on one of these three topics, and the

girl will start talking <u>a</u> <u>mile</u> <u>a</u> <u>minite</u>. There! <u>Now</u> <u>the</u> <u>cat's</u> <u>out</u> <u>of</u> <u>the</u> <u>bag</u>! It's up to you!"

  The next day, Jack sat down next to a girl he'd admired. Both sat <u>like</u> <u>bumps</u> <u>on</u> <u>a</u> <u>log</u>. An

uncomfortable silence rained. <u>Trying</u> <u>to</u> <u>keep</u> <u>his</u> <u>head</u> <u>above</u> <u>water</u>, Jack tried the first topic: rela-

tives. "Do you have any sisters?" he asked.

  "No," she replied, looking straight ahead.

<u>Taking</u> <u>the</u> <u>bull</u> <u>by</u> <u>the</u> <u>horns</u>, Jack tried again to <u>get</u> <u>the</u> <u>ball</u> <u>rolling</u>

with the second topic: food. "Do you like pizza?" he asked.

  "No," she replied.

<u>Feeling</u> <u>his</u> <u>ship</u> <u>going</u> <u>down</u>, Jack made one last attempt, <u>like</u> <u>a</u> <u>drowning</u> <u>man</u> <u>who</u> <u>clutches</u>

<u>at</u> <u>every</u> <u>twig</u>. <u>Jumping</u> <u>out</u> <u>of</u> <u>the</u> <u>frying</u> <u>pan</u> <u>into</u> <u>the</u> <u>fire</u>, he tried the third topic: philosophy.

"Well, if you had any sisters, do you think they wood like pizza?" he asked.

SPELLING BOX	1. _____	2. _____
3. _____	4. _____	5. _____

30. Practice Your Style
31. More Stylish Review
32. Perfect Your Style
33. Where's the Proof ?

Background Information

These exercises are a review of the concepts presented in Exercises 22–29.

Exercises 30, 31, and 32 involve choosing the mistake made in each sentence from a list of possible errors. Then each story is to be rewritten. You may wish to omit the rewriting of the stories if time does not permit.

Exercise 33 requires the students to mark each sentence correct or incorrect. Students must then rewrite each incorrect sentence correctly.

Answer Key for Exercise 30

Rewritten versions will vary. A suggested version follows. The misspelled words are *tomorrow, icy, their, weather,* and *believe.*

The local weatherman was doing his daily spot on the 5:00 P.M. newscast. He had startling news. "Tomorrow it will be cold, snowy, windy, and icy. A winter storm warning is in effect tonight and tomorrow. Cars will have trouble running. It will be a good night to stay indoors. There is a 90 percent chance that 2 feet of snow will fall in the next 2 hours. In order that we may keep roads clear for emergency vehicles, we suggest you stay home from work tonight and tomorrow. You'll be much safer and more comfortable."

Many listeners were looking outside while their weatherman was talking. The weather was great, 70 degrees with clear skies. The next morning dawned equally fair and warm.

Complaints poured in. The weatherman said to his boss, "I believe I would like a transfer." Asked why, he replied, "The climate here just doesn't agree with me."

1. c	4. b	7. e
2. d	5. e	8. f
3. a	6. f	9. c

Answer Key for Exercise 31

Rewritten versions will vary. A suggested version follows. The misspelled words are *principal, suburb, anxious, sputtered,* and *tried.*

1. d	5. b	9. b
2. e	6. d	10. f
3. f	7. e	
4. a	8. c	

Mr. Young had just been hired as principal of a prep school in a wealthy suburb. He was very anxious to make a good impression by seeing that everything was exactly right for his students.

On the first day of school, Mr. Young met two cafeteria workers. They were carrying a large soup kettle from the kitchen.

"Excuse me," said he. "May I have a taste of that, please?"

"But, sir . . ." began the workers.

"Now, look here! I don't want to hear it! Run to the kitchen and get me a spoon!"

One kitchen worker ran to the kitchen and returned with a spoon. Mr. Young dipped in the spoon, took a large swallow, turned green, and began to shake.

"You must be crazy!" he sputtered. "We can't serve that soup to our students!"

"No, Mr. Young, we tried to tell you. That's not soup! It's the dishwater!"

Answer Key for Exercise 32

The rewritten stories will vary. A suggested version is given below. The misspelled words are *two, aunt's, settling, frantic,* and *attention.*

1. a	4. e	7. f
2. a	5. d	8. b
3. f	6. c	9. f

A teenage girl was baby-sitting a three-year-old boy and a five-year-old girl. The children, who were not very well behaved, had been noisy all afternoon.

The baby-sitter had been instructed to take the children on the bus to their <u>aunt's</u> house across town at 3:00 P.M. She arrived at the bus stop just in time and settled down on the bus with the youngsters.

The baby-sitter took out a book. She told the five-year-old to watch the three-year-old. She said she wanted quiet to read her book.

The three-year-old became wild and didn't mind the older child. He ran, kicked, and shouted, to everyone's annoyance. Finally, most of the people got off the bus. The five-year-old became frantic, pulling at the baby-sitter's arm and trying to get her attention in every way possible. The baby-sitter ignored the child.

At last, the sitter shut the book and sighed, "That's it. Whatever do you want, child? And where is your brother?"

"That's what I tried to tell you. He got off a long way back with all those people!"

Answer Key for Exercise 33

Answers will vary. Here is one correct example for each sentence. Words that were misspelled have been underlined and rewritten correctly. They are *lapping, their, alligators, beckoned,* and *running.*

1. Incorrect. Deciding to spend spring vacation in Florida, the three college boys drove all night.
2. Incorrect. Twenty-four hours later they arrived in Daytona Beach exhausted.
3. Incorrect. But when they saw the blue waves <u>lapping</u> at the beautiful white beach, the boys decided they could sleep later.
4. Incorrect. They ripped off <u>their</u> shoes, took off their shirts, and got ready to dive in.
5. Incorrect. They saw no sharp rocks, sea anemones, or jellyfish.
6. Incorrect. One of the boys asked a local, "Do any <u>alligators</u> live around here?"
7. Correct.
8. Incorrect. The water <u>beckoned</u> invitingly to the boys, and they didn't wait another minute.
9. Incorrect. With a <u>running</u> start, they dove into the water.
10. Correct.

30. Practice Your Style

Directions: Each sentence below contains one major error. Write the letter of the error next to the sentence. You will use some letters more than once. Then circle the five misspelled words and rewrite each word correctly in the Spelling Box. Finally, rewrite the story, correcting each error. Use the back of this page or another piece of paper.

Errors

 a. The sentence is too wordy.

 b. The sentence contains clichés.

 c. The verb tense is not consistent.

 d. Sentences do not vary in length and form.

 e. It is a sentence fragment.

 f. These are run-on sentences.

_____   1. The local weatherman was doing his daily spot on the 5:00 P.M. newscast. He has startling news.

_____   2. "Tomorow it will be cold. It will be snowy. It will be windy. It will be icey."

_____   3. "A fierce, cold, terrible winter storm warning is in effect for tonight, Saturday, March 16, this very night, and for tomorrow."

_____   4. "Cars will be running slower than molasses in January. It will be a night fit for neither man nor beast."

_____   5. "A 90 percent chance that 2 feet of snow will fall in the next 2 hours."

_____   6. "In order that we may keep roads clear for emergency vehicles we suggest you stay home from work tonight and tomorrow you'll be much safer and more comfortable."

_____   7. Looking outside while there weatherman was talking.

_____   8. The whether was great, 70 degrees with clear skies, the next morning dawned equally fair and warm.

_____   9. Complaints poured in. The weatherman says to his boss, "I beleive I would like a transfer." Asked why, he replied, "The climate here just doesn't agree with me."

SPELLING BOX	1. _____	2. _____
3. _____	4. _____	5. _____

      Find the Errors!

31. More Stylish Review

Directions: Each sentence below contains one major error. Write the letter of that one error by the sentence. You will use some letters more than once. Then circle the five misspelled words, and rewrite each word correctly in the Spelling Box. Finally, rewrite the story, correcting each error. Use the back of this page or another piece of paper.

Errors

a. The sentence is too wordy.

b. The sentence contains clichés.

c. The verb tense is not consistent.

d. Sentences do not vary in length and form.

e. It is a sentence fragment.

f. These are run-on sentences.

_____ 1. Mr. Young had just been hired. He was hired as principle. He was principal of a prep school. The school was in a wealthy suberb.

_____ 2. Very anxous to make a good impression by seeing that everything was exactly right for his students.

_____ 3. On the first day of school, Mr. Young met two cafeteria workers they were carrying a large soup kettle from the kitchen.

_____ 4. "Excuse me, please. I beg your pardon," said he. "May I please have a wee little taste of that if you don't mind, please?"

_____ 5. "But sir . . ." began the workers, as quietly as mice.

_____ 6. "Now, look here! I don't want to hear it! Run to the kitchen. Run get me a spoon."

_____ 7. One kitchen worker running to the kitchen and returning with a spoon.

_____ 8. Mr. Young dips in the spoon, takes a large swallow, turned green, and began to shake.

_____ 9. "You must have bats in your belfry!" he sputered. "We can't serve that soup to our students!"

_____ 10. "No, Mr. Young, we tryed to tell you that's not soup it's the dishwater!"

SPELLING BOX	1. _____	2. _____
3. _____	4. _____	5. _____

32. Perfect Your Style

Directions: Each sentence below contains one major error. Write the letter of the error next to the sentence. You will use some letters more than once. Then circle the five misspelled words and rewrite each word correctly in the Spelling Box. Finally, rewrite the story, correcting each error. Use the back of this page or another piece of paper.

Errors

a. The sentence is too wordy.

b. The sentence contains clichés.

c. The verb tense is not consistent.

d. Sentences do not vary in length and form.

e. It is a sentence fragment.

f. These are run-on sentences.

_____ 1. A teenage girl was baby-sitting too small preschool children ages three and five, a three-year-old boy and a five-year-old girl.

_____ 2. The children, who were not very well behaved, had been noisy, loud and yelling all afternoon.

_____ 3. The baby-sitter had been instructed to take the children on the bus to their ant's house at 3:00 P.M. the aunt lived across town.

_____ 4. Arriving at the bus stop just in time and setling down with the youngsters.

_____ 5. The baby-sitter took out a book. She spoke to the five-year-old. She said to watch the three-year-old. She said she wanted to read her book. She wanted quiet.

_____ 6. The three-year-old became wild and doesn't mind the older child. The three-year-old ran and kicks and shouts, to everyone's annoyance.

_____ 7. Finally, most of the people got off the bus, the five-year-old became frantik pulling at the baby-sitter's arm trying to get her atention in every way possible she ignored the child.

_____ 8. At last, the sitter shut the book and sighed, "That's the straw that broke the camel's back. Whatever do you want, child? And where is your brother?"

_____ 9. "That's what I tried to tell you he got off a long way back with all those people!"

SPELLING BOX	1. _____	2. _____
3. _____	4. _____	5. _____

 Find the Errors!

33. Where's the Proof?

Directions: Write CORRECT or INCORRECT next to each sentence below. (Incorrect sentences may have these errors: wordiness, clichés, inconsistent verb tense, no variety in length or form of sentences, sentence fragment, or run-on sentence.) If the sentence is incorrect, rewrite it correctly in the space below the sentence. Circle the five misspelled words and spell each word correctly as you rewrite the sentences. Then write each corrected word in the Spelling Box.

_____ 1. Deciding to spend spring vacation in Florida, the car was driven all night by the three college boys.

_____ 2. Twenty-four hours later they arrived in Daytona Beach the next day, tired, exhausted, and completely worn out.

_____ 3. But when they saw the blue waves laping at the beautiful white beach, the boys decided haste makes waste.

_____ 4. They ripped off thier shoes. They took off their shirts. They got ready. They prepared to dive in.

_____ 5. Seeing no sharp rocks, sea anemones, or jellyfish.

_____ 6. One of the boys thought about aligators asked a local, "Do any alligators live around here?"

_____ 7. The local answered, "Of course not!"

_____ 8. The water beckens invitingly to the boys, and they didn't wait another minute.

_____ 9. With a runing start dove into the water.

_____ 10. "The sharks chase the alligators away!" the local continued.

SPELLING BOX	1. _____	2. _____
3. _____	4. _____	5. _____

34. School Daze

Background Information

This exercise is a review of capitalization and punctuation. There may be some disagreement about the inclusion of exclamation points after some sentences. Allow for variation unless the exclamation is clearly called for by the sense of the sentence.

Answer Key

Each joke has been rewritten correctly below. Each misspelled word has been underlined and rewritten correctly in the text of the joke. The misspelled words are *tongue, equation, snapping, picture,* and *difference.*

1. Chemistry Teacher: What is HNO_3?
    Student: Oh, I've got it! It's right on the tip of my tongue!
    Teacher: Well, you'd better spit it out!
    It's nitric acid!

2. Teacher: Why don't you ever know the answers to any of my questions?
    Student: If I did, what would be the use of my coming here?

3. Teacher (finishing long algebra equation): Thus, we find that the answer is zero.
    Student (snapping shut textbook Basic Algebra): Gee, all that work for nothing!

4. Student: I was the smartest one in the seventh grade today, Mom.
    Mom: Oh, why was that?
    Student: Miss Gaston asked each of us to draw our favorite part of the book Hansel and Gretel. Then the class had to guess what it was. Mine was the only picture no one could guess, but I knew what it was all along.

5. Math Teacher: Take 114 $\frac{9}{16}$ from 209 $\frac{1}{4}$, and what's the difference?
    Student: That's what I say! It doesn't make any difference to me!

34. School Daze

Directions: Proofread each joke below, and make any corrections in capitalization or punctuation that are needed. Do not add any quotation marks. Circle the five misspelled words, and rewrite each word correctly in the Spelling Box.

1. Chemistry Teacher: What is HNO_3

   Student: Oh Ive got it Its right on the tip of my tonge

   Chemistry Teacher: Well youd better spit it out Its nitric acid

2. Teacher: Why dont you ever know the answers to any of my questions

   Student: If I did what would be the use of my coming here

3. Teacher (finishing long algebra eqation): Thus we find that the answer is zero.

   Student (snaping shut textbook basic algebra): Gee all that work for nothing

4. Student: I was the smartest one in the seventh grade today mom

   Mom: Oh why was that

   Student: Miss Gaston asked each of us to draw our favorite part of the book hansel and

   gretel. then the class had to guess what it was. mine was the only pitcher no one could

   guess but i knew what it was all along

5. Math Teacher: Take $114\frac{9}{16}$ from $209\frac{1}{4}$ and whats the diffrence

   Student: Thats what i say it doesnt make any difference to me

SPELLING BOX	1. _____	2. _____
3. _____	4. _____	5. _____

Find the Errors!

35. Proofreader's Delight
36. Positively Proofread!

Background Information

These exercises are a review of all the concepts presented in *Find the Errors!*

Answer Key for Exercise 35

Answers will vary somewhat. A suggested corrected version of the story is given below. Words misspelled in the original story have been underlined and rewritten in the text. The misspelled words are *scholarly, history, skillful, happened,* and *delight.*

The teacher of American History I, Mr. Wilson, was a scholarly gentleman but quite beloved by his students. His history classes were very popular with the sophomore students at Wingfield High School.

Mr. Wilson's class used the text *Fascinating American History.* But Mr. Wilson was especially skillful at telling interesting stories which really made American history come alive for the students.

Mr. Wilson's only fault was a tendency to become long-winded. One hot Monday afternoon in October, which happened to be Columbus Day, Mr. Wilson was telling the story of the Nina, the Pinta, and the Santa Maria. As he rambled on, he lost his place in his notes for the third or fourth time. "Now, where was I?" he asked in confusion.

To the delight of the class, and Mr. Wilson as well, one student spoke up and said, "In conclusion!"

Answer Key for Exercise 36

Answers will vary somewhat. A suggested version follows. Words misspelled in the original have been underlined and rewritten correctly. The misspelled words are *roll, course, here, grammar,* and *embarrassing.*

It was a beautiful, sunny day in April, right before spring vacation. The teacher was calling the roll in English Composition I, a freshman course at Woodville Junior High School.

Two students were absent. The teacher asked the class, "Won't Ginny and Jill be here this afternoon?"

Another girl in the class (who was always very truthful) answered, "Jill said that Ginny and she were going home to 'lay in the sun.'"

Trying to correct the girl's grammar without embarrassing her, the teacher went over and whispered, "Lie!"

The girl was astonished. "OK," she replied. "Ginny and she went to visit Ginny's aunt in Hong Kong today and won't be back until after class."

Additional Activities for Exercises 35–36

1. Construct additional paragraphs in which you make various errors of the types studied in *Find the Errors!* Have students rewrite the paragraphs correctly.

2. Have students write original paragraphs. Instruct them to proofread their own paragraphs using the Proofreading Checklist, looking specifically for the types of errors studied in *Find the Errors!*

35. Proofreader's Delight

Directions: The story below has been separated into four sections. Rewrite each section, making all corrections necessary. There may be errors in capitalization, punctuation, or verb usage. You may find sentence fragments, run-on sentences, wordy sentences, clichés, inconsistent verb tenses, or sentences that do not vary in length or form. Circle the five misspelled words, and rewrite each word correctly as you rewrite the story. Then write each corrected word in the Spelling Box.

The teacher of american history I mr wilson, was a schoolarly gentleman but quite beloved by his students. His histry classes was very popular with the Sophomore students at wingfield high school.

Mr wilsons class used the text fascinating american history. But mr. wilson was especially good and skilful at telling interesting stories which really interested the students and held their attention made american history come alive.

Mr wilson's only fault was a tendency to become long-winded and talk on and on and occasionally some of his lectures were just too long. One hot monday afternoon in october which hapened to be columbus day mr wilson was telling at great length the story of the nina the pinta and the santa maria. As he rambles on he lost his place in his notes for the third or fourth time. Now where was I he asks in confusion.

To the delite of the class and mr wilson as well one student spoke up and said in conclusion.

SPELLING BOX	1. _____	2. _____
3. _____	4. _____	5. _____

36. Positively Proofread!

Directions: The story below has been separated into four sections. Rewrite each section, making all corrections necessary. Look for errors in capitalization, punctuation, or verb usage. You may also find sentence fragments, run-on sentences, wordy sentences, clichés, inconsistent verb tenses, or sentences that do not vary in length or form. Circle the five misspelled words, and spell each word correctly as you rewrite the story.

It was a beautiful sunny day in april right before Spring Vacation. The weather was nice. The teacher was calling the role in english composition I a freshman coarse in english composition at woodville junior high school.

two students was absent. The teacher asks the class wont ginny and jill be hear this afternoon

another girl in the class (who was always very truthful), answered, jill said that her and ginny was going home to 'lay in the sun.' Trying to correct the girls grammer without embarassing her the teacher went over and whispered, "lie"

The girl was astonished. OK she replied her and ginny went to visit ginnys aunt in hong kong today and wont be back until after class.

Find the Errors!

37. Proofreading Crossword Puzzle

Background Information

This crossword puzzle will help students review the terms presented in *Find the Errors!*

Answer Key

Across

1. underlined
2. variety
3. apostrophe
4. comma

5. hyphen
6. run-on
7. principal

8. verb
9. cliché
10. wordy
11. colon

Down

2. vocabulary
7. period
13. tense
14. fragment
15. pronoun

16. question
17. proper
18. proofreading
19. exclamation

37. Proofreading Crossword Puzzle

Directions: Complete the crossword puzzle using the clues below. Each clue refers to a word studied in *Find the Errors!*

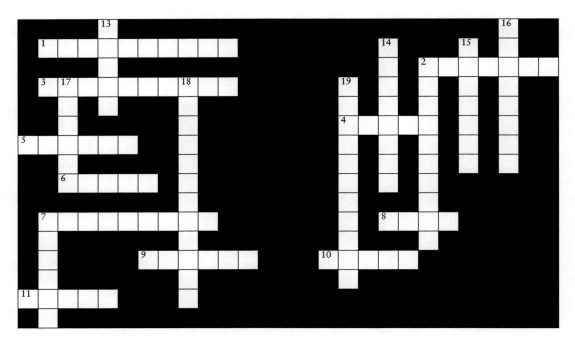

Across

1. Names of books should be u_____.
2. Try to have _____ in length and form of your sentences.
3. This mark is used to make a word possessive.
4. This mark is used to separate items in a series.
5. This mark is used to divide a word at the end of a line.
6. Sentences that run together without punctuation are _____ sentences.
7. The four basic forms of a verb are its _____ parts.
8. The subject and _____ must agree.
9. An overused expression is a _____.
10. A repetitious, overwritten sentence is _____.
11. This mark is used to mean "as follows."

Down

2. Substitute lively _____ for boring, "tired" words.
7. This is used after an abbreviation.
13. Verb _____ must be consistent.
14. A sentence _____ is an incomplete thought.
15. *I, she,* and *he* are examples of this part of speech.
16. This ends an interrogative sentence: a _____ mark.
17. Capitalize _____ nouns and adjectives.
18. Careful_____ will improve your written work.
19. This mark is used to show excitement: an _____ point.

76   *Find the Errors!*

Find the Errors! Posttest

Background Information

See comments for Exercise 1, the pretest for *Find the Errors!*

Answer Key

Words misspelled in the test have been underlined and corrected. They are *sophomore, scholarship, chocolate, sincerely, popular, varieties, it's, its, a lot,* and *committee.*

1. Hector said that he hoped to go to <u>S</u>anta <u>R</u>osa <u>J</u>unior <u>C</u>ollege to major in <u>H</u>ispanic studies.

2. Chico said, "<u>I</u>n <u>E</u>dith <u>H</u>amilton's book <u>Mythology</u> you will read about the god <u>Z</u>eus and the goddess <u>D</u>emeter, among others."

3. Jess is taking chemistry<u>,</u> <u>S</u>panish<u>,</u> accounting<u>,</u> and <u>A</u>merican history in his <u>sophomore</u> year at <u>M</u>urrah <u>H</u>igh <u>S</u>chool.

4. Joy's <u>F</u>rench horn teacher is <u>Dr.</u> Perry <u>I.</u> Combs<u>,</u> <u>J</u>r.

5. Lloyd won a full <u>scholarship</u> to <u>H</u>inds <u>J</u>unior <u>C</u>ollege.

6. "OK<u>,</u> I'll go<u>,</u>" said Joel<u>,</u> "if you want me to."

7. The <u>A</u>merican water spaniel has curly<u>,</u> <u>choco-late</u>-brown hair.

8. Esther tried out for the soccer team<u>,</u> and she was surprised when she made it.

9. She signed the letter, "<u>Sincerely</u>, Ms. <u>J.</u> <u>T.</u> Peatross."

10. A nine<u>-</u>tenths majority of the voters supported the ex<u>-</u>football player in his bid for office.

11. Flights from this airport to cities in Mexico <u>are</u> <u>popular</u> with vacationers.

12. This rose, unlike many other <u>varieties</u>, <u>is</u> fast<u>-</u>growing.

13. <u>It's</u> time to feed the dog<u>,</u> or it will start barking for <u>its</u> food.

14. After class Miss Bryan<u>,</u> our <u>F</u>rench teacher<u>,</u> gave Maya<u>,</u> Lex<u>,</u> and <u>me</u> some help with our translations.

15. While I was playing tennis, I sprained my ankle. (Answers may vary. Accept any reasonable answer.)

16. A great party, with <u>a</u> <u>lot</u> of food and drink and a great band for dancing, <u>is</u> <u>planned</u> <u>for</u> <u>Labor</u> <u>Day</u>. (Answers will vary. Accept any reasonable answer.)

17. Jose Tores, Michael Wilson, Jenny French, and Kathryn Walden are running for class president.

18. Jake kicked the ball hard, and it narrowly <u>missed</u> the goal. OR: Jake <u>kicks</u> the ball hard, and it narrowly misses the goal.

19. My opinion won't count when the <u>committee</u> decides where the party will be. (Answers will vary. The word *irregardless* is always incorrect and should definitely be eliminated. The words *what I think* and *my opinion* are repetitious; one or the other should be eliminated. The phrase *where it will be at* is incorrect; the word *at* must be eliminated.)

20. The week before exams, Hal was either very busy or very worried as he studied hard. (Answers will vary. Students should eliminate the clichés *busy as a bee, depths of despair,* and *crystal clear.*

Find the Errors! Posttest

Directions: Each sentence below has several major errors. The errors may be in capitalization, punctuation, or verb usage. You may find sentence fragments, run-on sentences, wordy sentences, clichés, or inconsistent verb tenses. There may be dangling or misplaced modifiers or incorrect pronouns.

Rewrite each sentence correctly in the space below it. There are also 10 misspelled words in this test. Circle these 10 words and rewrite them correctly as you rewrite the sentences. (Missing capital letters do not count as misspelled words.)

1. Hector said that he hoped to go to santa rosa junior college to major in hispanic studies.

2. Chico said, "in edith hamilton's book mythology you will read about the god zeus and the goddess demeter, among others."

3. Jess is taking chemistry spanish accounting and american history in his sophmore year at murrah high school.

4. Joy's french horn teacher is dr perry j combs jr.

5. Lloyd won a full scholership to hinds junior college.

6. "OK I'll go" said Joel "if you want me to."

(continued)

Find the Errors! **Posttest** *(continued)*

7. The american water spaniel has curly choclate brown hair.

8. Esther tried out for the soccer team and she was surprised when she made it.

9. She signed the letter, "Sincerly, Ms J T Peatross."

10. A nine tenths majority of the voters supported the ex football player in his bid for office.

11. Flights from this airport to cities in Mexico is populer with vacationers.

12. This rose, unlike many other varietys, are fast growing.

13. Its time to feed the dog or it will start barking for it's food.

(continued)

Find the Errors! Posttest *(continued)*

14. After class Miss Bryan our french teacher gave Maya Lex and I some help with our translations.

15. Playing tennis my ankle was sprained.

16. A great party with alot of food and drink and a great band for dancing!

17. Jose Tores is running for class president. Michael Wilson is running too. Also Jenny French is running. And Kathryn Walden is running.

18. Jake kicked the ball hard, and it narrowly misses the goal.

19. Irregardless of what I may think, my opinion won't count when the comittee decides on where the party will be at.

20. The week before exams, Hal was either busy as a bee or in the depths of despair as he worked to make his studies crystal clear.

Proofreading Checklist

Background Information

The reproducible checklist on page 82 provides students with a guide to check their own writing for errors. You may wish to assign several short writing assignments and have students proofread their own work using this checklist.

Proofreading Checklist

Directions: Refer to this checklist whenever you write a paper for any class. Check the list carefully to see that you have proofread correctly and have caught all errors.

I. MECHANICS

I have checked to see that . . .

1. Capital letters are used whenever needed.

2. End punctuation is correct for each sentence.

3. Commas are used only as necessary.

4. Direct quotations are enclosed in quotation marks.

5. Colons, hyphens, apostrophes, and underlining or italics are included where needed.

6. All subjects and verbs agree.

7. Correct principal parts of verbs are used.

8. Pronouns are used correctly.

9. There are no spelling errors.

II. STYLE

I have checked to see that . . .

10. Dangling or misplaced modifiers have been avoided.

11. Run-on sentences and sentence fragments have been eliminated.

12. Sentences vary in length and form.

13. Verb tense is consistent throughout.

14. Tired, boring words have been replaced by lively vocabulary.

15. Wordy sentences have been simplified.

16. No clichés were used.

17. An unnatural, overwritten style (too many big words, foreign words, and flowery sentences) has been avoided.

18. This writing is logical, orderly, well organized, and interesting.

19. This writing represents my best effort.

Notes

Notes

Notes

Share Your Bright Ideas with Us!

We want to hear from you! Your valuable comments and suggestions will help us meet your current and future classroom needs.

Your name_____Date_____

School name_____

School address_____

City _____State _____Zip_____Phone number (_____)_____

Grade level taught_____Subject area(s) taught_____Average class size_____

Where did you purchase this publication?_____

Was your salesperson knowledgeable about this product?   Yes_____   No_____

What monies were used to purchase this product?

____School supplemental budget   ____Federal/state funding   ____Personal

Please "grade" this Walch publication according to the following criteria:

Quality of service you received when purchasing .... A   B   C   D   F
Ease of use.. A   B   C   D   F
Quality of content... A   B   C   D   F
Page layout .... A   B   C   D   F
Organization of material .... A   B   C   D   F
Suitability for grade level .... A   B   C   D   F
Instructional value.. A   B   C   D   F

COMMENTS:_____

_____

What specific supplemental materials would help you meet your current—or future—instructional needs?

_____

Have you used other Walch publications? If so, which ones?_____

May we use your comments in upcoming communications?   ____Yes   ____No

Please **FAX** this completed form to **207-772-3105**, or mail it to:

Product Development, J. Weston Walch, Publisher, P. O. Box 658, Portland, ME 04104-0658

We will send you a **FREE GIFT** as our way of thanking you for your feedback. **THANK YOU!**